Rumors, Lies, and Whispers

Rumors, Lies, and Whispers

Classroom "Crush" or Career Catastrophe?

Mary Ann Manos

PRAEGER

Westport, Connecticut
London

Library of Congress Cataloging-in-Publication Data

Manos, Mary Ann, 1950–
   Rumors, lies, and whispers : classroom "crush" or career catastrophe? / Mary Ann Manos.
     p. cm.
   Includes bibliographical references and index.
   ISBN 0–275–97834–6 (alk. paper)
     1. Teachers—Complaints against—United States.   2. Child sexual abuse by teachers—
United States—Prevention.   3. Truthfulness and falsehood.   I. Title.
LB2844.1.C54M36   2004
371.1–dc22   2003062439

British Library Cataloguing in Publication Data is available.

Library of Congress Catalog Card Number: 2003062439
ISBN: 0–275–97834–6

First published in 2004

Praeger Publishers, 88 Post Road West, Westport, CT 06881
An imprint of Greenwood Publishing Group, Inc.
www.praeger.com

Printed in the United States of America

The paper used in this book complies with the
Permanent Paper Standard issued by the National
Information Standards Organization (Z39.48–1984).

10 9 8 7 6 5 4 3 2 1

Copyright Acknowledgment

Excerpts from *Black's Law Dictionary* by Henry Black (St. Paul, MN: West Publishing, 1979),
reprinted with permission.

My love and my appreciation go to my family for their encouragement and support throughout this time-consuming process:

My dearest husband, Ralph,
My daughters, Molly and April, and
My mother, Helen Mae.

CONTENTS

INTRODUCTION

A confiscated candy bar began the research for this book.

One day during second period, an eighth-grade girl argued with her social studies teacher about a candy bar she had been directed to put in her book bag. The minor confrontation ended with the candy bar resting in the teacher's desk. The next day, the girl and her mother appeared in the principal's office—not to regain the candy bar, but to accuse the teacher of inappropriate behavior. They alleged the male teacher had touched the girl in a sexual manner. That report began the rush to judgment that resulted in the young professional's resignation.

Although an allegation of sexual misconduct is a terrible situation for any teacher, those who are proactive and know their legal rights are better prepared to hold onto their jobs and reputations. Teachers are the focus of this text. The information I include is presented for their welfare. Thirty years of working in schools and learning about classrooms and teachers did not prepare me for the knowledge I would gain about teacher sexual misconduct. The swift rush to judgment shocked even a classroom veteran like me.

Americans are painfully aware of the headlines that sensationalize teacher-student sexual trysts. Certainly, I found such cases in newspaper accounts across the county. On the other hand, I know that many teachers fail to realize the importance of such an allegation to their continued teaching career, until they experience it. Unfortunately, few are aware of the myriad cases of alleged teacher sexual misconduct that are completely unfounded. Sadly, I cannot say *proven* unfounded, because in most cases no proof is ever sought out. Within hours of such an allegation the teacher leaves with a destroyed reputation and a loss of career and livelihood.

The mere whisper of sexual taint in classroom behavior slams the teacher with suspicion, silence, and presumed guilt. The few hours in the wake of an allegation are critical to the survival of a fine teaching career. The community, school administrators, and students play powerful parts in such a drama. In the face of withering criticism, even experienced, tenured teachers shrink from standing up for themselves. They often know little regarding their legal rights. Extracurricular teachers, who often spend many hours outside the classroom with students in many settings, are most at risk for such allegations.

Most teachers are simply not prepared for the vehement onslaught of personal criticism. This criticism strikes to the heart of teachers and they fold under the intense pressure. Unfortunately, the accused teachers are powerless to provide any self-defense other than resignation. Even that drastic step adds to the implication that they are guilty. Further, new legislation in many states mandates all resignations rendered under surmise of inappropriate sexual behavior be reported to state boards of education or other agencies that publish lists via the Internet. A teaching career is ended in public shame.

Skeptics will say it is better to remove any teacher in question, but they fail to realize the impact of an emotional accusation made as a result of adolescent anger, parental gold digging, or political reprisal. Parents and community members rush to the defense of the student in question, touting a loss of innocence due to teacher sexual assault or abuse. Although that may be the case in some situations, more often the students know the allegation is untrue. Further, they garner support from classmates who continue the lie, buffeted with additional details (some of which are simply impossible or fantastic in nature). Once the lie is publicized, the path is clear. Parents who have an axe to grind add to the fracas with emotional and perhaps irrelevant information. The school administration often adds fuel to the fire through intense silence, wild rumors, or quotes taken out of context. The converging factors conspire against cool heads. The conspicuous absence of the accused teacher lends itself to escalation of the situation. The community wants answers and a clear view of the public punishment.

Most teachers know nothing of the frequency of false allegations; neither do they have knowledge or skills that would help them be proactive in highly charged settings. Colleges of education fail to present essential information about avoiding questionable behavior. Education books on class management rarely explain helpful methods on dealing with the classroom crush (the one source of problematic behavior that can be anticipated by the teachers). School administrators rarely have employees trained in Title IX sexual harassment issues available for teachers to consult. Few districts plan and implement yearly seminars. Teacher professional unions may offer no legal support for teachers in the mire of alleged sexual misconduct, which is considered a criminal offense as opposed to a contractual grievance. When a school district or teacher association attorney proffers clear warnings for teachers to stay out of isolated situations or to refrain from touching students, they are met with scoffing from the faculty. Why? Because teachers may be the only adults the students have on their side emotionally. The closeness of the student-teacher relationship engenders hugs, pats on the back, and frequent physical contact. Imposing a cool distance between teachers and students flies in the face of dedicated, caring teachers. In short, warnings of alleged misconduct are either absent or go unheeded.

Professionals must be aware of the potential signs of student infatuation. Teachers must also be informed as to the events that will inevitably happen in cases of alleged sexual misconduct. I have gone further than simply telling faculty not to touch students. I provide response steps for accurate documentation of educator personal and professional recordkeeping, how to handle parent conferences, and how to foresee and react to situations designed by parents who seek monetary settlements from the school district. Most important, I walk teachers through each step of the criminal and professional investigation, to empower their decision making.

All teachers must discuss and problem-solve such situations, enabling them to think ahead. Perhaps more important, colleges of education must prepare teacher candidates with the skills to identify and intervene in problematic student behavior and how to avoid the appearance of wrongdoing. Our most trusting, young professionals are the most at risk. Often, young teachers are swept into the maelstrom.

They effectively lose a career investment of thousands of dollars in a few moments.

In this book, I attempt to facilitate the institutional introspection that impacts school district policy formulation. Teachers and school administrators must begin to look at the possibility of a wrongful allegation through the lens of federal guidelines, school policy, and professional behavior constraints. Although teacher sexual misconduct is a criminal charge, several civil cases deal with ancillary issues such as negligent hiring, negligent supervision, gross and deliberate indifference, "Color of law" torts, the "Shocks the conscience" standard, and federal Title IX guidelines. Further, I offer several ideas to provide effective teacher in-service. Finally, school administrators who are aware of potential liabilities can be proactive in scheduling and personnel assignment. Added to and superseded by all of the above factors must be a strong sense of democratic justice. That is, a teacher must be proven guilty, not simply presumed guilty.

Finally, and perhaps most important, several scenarios are provided for discussion. Teacher sexual misconduct is often the topic of hushed conversation, after the fact. On the other hand, the time frame for effective discussion is before the situation arrives. School administrators may not want to broach the topic, fearing equipping a teacher with advance knowledge of the process. How foolish on their part! Excellent teachers caught up in the nightmare do not get a second chance at a career. Why not help good teachers think through the situation before they are faced with it?

The most elusive research aspect of this text was the "silent statistic." That is, teachers who choose to leave their careers rather than fight the allegations. They are often trusted teachers with fine reputations. What happened? Were they really closet pedophiles who managed to hide monstrous actions until unmasked by a few brave students? Or could the reality involve teachers who unknowingly put themselves in harm's way through poor decision making? This silent statistic, or the number of teachers who simply resign without a fight, causes me much concern. In the few literature sources available, authors seem to agree. They concede a few wrongful allegations may exist, but estimate it rarely happens. I disagree heartily. Based on 30 years of teaching experience in several states, I can honestly state three truths: students often see things much differently than adults; parents may hold motivation other than a child's welfare; and finally, school administrators dislike controversy. These are the three core elements in an allegation of sexual misconduct, and they are volatile when mixed. The silent statistic of the number of teachers who leave faculty positions due to wrongful allegation of sexual misconduct is shocking.

I hope this text helps to inform and prepare all professionals who work with children. It will equip teachers with a survival plan, descriptors of problematic student behavior, pertinent law cases, school policies, and criminal investigation procedures, all discussed within a context of teacher advocacy. The intent of this book is not to document the investigation of a pedophile masquerading as a teacher, rather it is to describe a teacher wrongfully accused of sexual misconduct. A book like this is long overdue and should be required reading in all colleges of education. Indeed, all professionals who work with children should read and remember the contents of this text.

A "candy bar" postscript: The teacher was immediately suspended and resigned within 48 hours. The student recanted the story within a week's time. The parent commented to the principal that she didn't want the teacher to be fired; she just expected an offer of money from the school district to forget the entire situation. No action was taken against the student or parent.

Dr. Mary Ann Manos

CHAPTER 1

A Sign of the Times

■■■

OVERVIEW

This chapter will describe the social and educational context for false allegations of teacher sexual misconduct. Although hindered by a dearth of educational research in regard to false allegations, practicing educators know that classroom reality often conflicts with research. The chapter will conclude with a call for teachers to provide research documentation by sharing their classroom experiences.

■■■

OBJECTIVES

After completing this chapter, the reader should be able to:

1. Describe U.S. Department of Justice crime survey reports of sexual assault in schools.
2. Identify media influences on school-age students' self-images and peer interactions.

■■■

WHO MIGHT BE FALSELY ACCUSED OF SEXUAL MISCONDUCT?

Television stations often broadcast disturbing pictures to the public. In one case, a reporter interviewed an eighth-grade teacher who was accused of improper conduct. The alleged incident happened during an overnight school lock-in. A middle-level student reported that the teacher had kissed her. She volunteered another middle school student as her witness. In an attempt to quiet community reaction, the school district immediately suspended the second-year teacher. Within hours, the teacher submitted his resignation. Although the following week both students recanted their stories, the incident left the young professional angry and in a tenuous employment situation. He did not return to the district. Local TV cameras recorded his last poignant statement, "I just want to tell other teachers that this can happen to you."

Make no mistake about it—this book is written for teachers, child-care workers, and school counselors. It is a basic survival course for those who wish to stay out of court for alleged sexual misconduct. News headlines shrill accounts of teachers who are accused of misconduct, but no one knows how many careers have been falsely maligned and ended by students who intend retribution for many reasons—extortion, revenge, misplaced affection, or sheer malice. No data or studies have documented the extent of the problem. Accused educators become a silent statistic due to the stigma of shame surrounding such an allegation.

A few experts say false allegations never happen; others say the situation rarely happens. Talk to classroom teachers and school administrators—they know it happens quite often. Most can even tell you which students sexually harass male and female teachers alike. Teachers know such an accusation is the death knell to an otherwise stellar career. The most vulnerable teachers are the youngest professionals. Fresh-faced and idealistic, first-year teachers want to save the world. They see students as personal friends. Unsure about the boundaries of the teacher-student relationship, they often stray across professional limits of behavior. They end up defamed and embittered. Even the most experienced, stalwart, innocent teacher cannot withstand the flood of public opinion and surmise. Vilified, the accused teacher resigns. End of story.

■■

HOW COMMON ARE ALLEGATIONS OF TEACHER SEXUAL MISCONDUCT?

Nearly every author of published material regarding sexual abuse in the school environment agrees, however begrudgingly, that sexual harassment and false allegations of sexual misconduct toward teachers exist. But they disagree on how often such harassment happens in the regular classroom.

In fact, false allegations of teacher sexual misconduct do happen. You don't have to explain that to the assistant principal who lost his job because seven students made a pact to get him fired in revenge for past disciplinary actions.[1] Or ask the gym teacher who was accused of sexual misconduct by several girls disgruntled because he yelled at them during gym class.[2] Not convinced? What about the nine-year-old girl who paid classmates $1 each to accuse a substitute teacher of sexual abuse?[3] False allegations of teacher misconduct happen. A malicious student can make them happen with very little provocation.

Enter the terms "school" and "Lolita" into a Web search and you will find hundreds of recent newspaper headlines. Enter the same terms into a search of available education books and you will fail to find a single volume. Headlines from the United Kingdom, the United States, Australia, and Canada scream secondhand reports and rumors to the public. On the other hand, teachers, counselors, and school administrators who work with adolescents may *not even think* about student intent, experience, or knowledge level in regard to the classroom "crush." Yet schools and teachers often find themselves dealing with off-color comments from students as young as preschool age. Students who perform sexual gestures and share sexually explicit jokes can be found in elementary classrooms on a daily basis.

Only classroom teachers know the full impact of a false allegation. Such events test the mettle of school administrators, faculty colleagues, community members, and ultimately the court system. Justice Anne Gardner of the Texas Second District Court of Appeals writes, "Teachers are particularly vulnerable to fabrications by disgruntled students or parents . . . a teacher is just one false accusation away from losing his or her career."[4]

Few if any studies have investigated the question of sexual harassment toward school faculty. In one study conducted by the

American Association of University Women (AAUW), 36 percent of high school students reported that students do indeed sexually harass teachers and other school personnel. The AAUW's research concluded what nearly every survey and study shows—that sexual harassment is directed more often at women than men.[5] Informal conversations with classroom educators continue to affirm that girls and boys in secondary settings also harass male teachers. Teachers most at risk for harassment seem to be young professionals, women faculty,[6] and teachers of extended-day subjects such as athletics, music, art, and drama.[7]

■■■

ARE STUDENTS AWARE OF SEXUAL MESSAGES?

Children are surrounded by sexual images in our modern world. The mass media provides models of gratuitous aggression and detailed sexual behavior. Children watch and learn. From Madison Avenue to Hollywood Boulevard, children are introduced to clothing, music, and cosmetics advertising, TV shows, and movies that extol physical sexual experiences of young men and women. For example, MTV, a network that courts an audience share of 12- to 17-year-old consumers, has on its schedule *Undressed*, a soap opera showing high school and college students involved in sexual situations. One such episode centers on a stepbrother and stepsister involved in a sexual relationship.[8] Vivid, explicit language and sexual scenes provide unforgettable images for children as young as kindergarten age.

For many students, isolation from these images is impossible; for others, involvement in the culture is expected and/or encouraged by parents and peers. As early as elementary school, parents want to think their child is attractive, sometimes in a way more mature than the child's age would suggest. Due to an unexplained trend toward early puberty in females, girls as young as eight years old are experiencing puberty.[9] Children's clothing styles have taken on a decidedly adult tone. One recent newspaper article described trendy children's shops offering makeup, high heels, and bare-midriff clothing for eight-year-old children.[10] Students emulate TV behaviors. In fact, 64 percent of male students (grades 7–12) report they are strongly influenced by entertainment stars and professional athletes.[11] Additionally, music videos display professional dancers demonstrating suggestive dance steps that are mimicked by girls and boys across the nation. One has only to attend a middle school or high school dance to see the "humpty" dance. It is no mystery why students experience confusion about appropriate behavior in the classroom.

Students do not shed these images at the schoolhouse door. The classroom is not isolated from modern culture or media influence. The fantastic images of youth icons and music stars are splashed across school clothing, school locker decoration, paper folders, and notebooks.

Schools encourage students to watch in-school TV news programs tailored to youth interests. Such programs are accompanied by the same images seen on nationwide media, only now served to a captive audience of children at school desks. Early adolescents, enticed by sexual messages in the media, often bring fantasies into the public and private school classroom. It follows that some students exhibit inappropriate behavior toward peers, teachers, and other school personnel. Such confusion has deadly impact for the career of professional educators.

■■■

HOW COMMON IS SEXUAL HARASSMENT IN THE SCHOOL ENVIRONMENT?

Supreme Court Justice Sandra Day O'Connor writes, "Sexual harassment . . . is an all too common aspect of the educational experience."[12] In fact, students do exhibit sexually harassing behavior toward school faculty and peers. The U.S. Department of Justice tracks sexual assault, rape, and sexually oriented verbal assault reports from selected school districts across the nation. Amazingly, in one year (1996–97) approximately 2,500 rapes, sexual assaults, or other sexual battery (*student to student*) were reported. Over 400 incidents were at the elementary school level. From 1995 to 1999, over 73,000 incidents of violence (which includes sexual battery and rape) *against teachers* were reported.[13] Furthermore, many incidents go unreported.

Kids will be kids. Unfortunately, children may also display the worst adult behavior. Sadly, many students and teachers are unable to identify peer-to-peer sexual harassment behaviors. According to the

Office of Civil Rights, a behavioral definition of sexual harassment would include:

1. Flipping up skirts
2. Shouting obscenities
3. Leaving obscene messages
4. Displaying pictures with sexual content
5. Writing notes or letters of a sexual nature
6. Spreading rumors about a person's sexual nature
7. Making humor or jokes about sex
8. Making sexual innuendoes in comments
9. Making phone calls of a sexual nature
10. Pulling down shorts[14]

Such behaviors are common occurrences in many middle and secondary school hallways and lunchrooms. Many children enjoy pushing the limits of acceptable behavior. From student art to published yearbooks, attempting to control sexual content is an ongoing battle for elementary and secondary teachers.

Why do students act out sexually harassing behaviors? Students, themselves, provide the following reasons:

1. "It's just part of school, it's no big deal." (39 percent)
2. They thought the person liked it. (28 percent)
3. They wanted a date with that person. (24 percent)
4. Their friends encouraged them to do it. (24 percent)

However, 81 percent of students surveyed reported they had been the recipients of sexual harassment at school. Over half of the students (54 percent) reported that they had been both harassers and harassed.[15] Furthermore, the number of girls and boys who have sexually harassed others is about equal (52.9 percent boys to 52.5 percent girls).[16] Clearly, sexual knowledge and overt sexual behaviors by students have increased in the past ten years. Although practicing classroom teachers will wholeheartedly agree, many are completely unprepared to become targets for inappropriate student behavior and sexually oriented comments.

■■■

THEY ARE JUST JOKING, AREN'T THEY?

Men and women educators respond differently to sexual harassment situations. The teacher's first response to sexual harassment from a student will differ considerably per gender. Although no studies have been conducted analyzing *teacher* response to sexual harassment, research describing gender differences in response to sexual harassment may give us an idea of what happens. Men tend to think of the harassing behavior as joking or as flattering. They ignore the behavior. Women tend to take a nonconfrontational stance such as talking to others to vent emotions, rather than confronting the harasser.[17] Common reasons sexual harassment is not reported include the following:

1. Victims feel helpless or embarrassed.
2. Victims think their complaint won't be taken seriously.
3. Victims don't trust their own perceptions of what happened.
4. Victims don't trust the system.
5. Victims don't think their school will support them if they report the harassment.
6. Victims are afraid of the harasser or his or her friends or family.[18]

All roads end in disaster for an educator being harassed by students. Hesitant teachers lose the opportunity to halt unwelcome behavior. The harasser always wins when the victim does nothing in response to hurtful or suggestive comments. Furthermore, in a court of law, silence on the teacher's part assumes acceptance and tacit approval of the student behavior.

There may not be any consequences for the underage student. As minors, students hold no legal responsibility for their actions. Should students make allegations and then recant, there is strong likelihood that *no* disciplinary action will be taken against them. No public apology is required because such an apology would dissuade other students from coming forth in case of an actual incident.[19] No fine is charged because schools cannot impose fines upon students for falsely reporting a crime. Police reports are made by the school district, not the student.[20] Any punishment meted out by school district officials will be slight. How slight? One school district merely tempo-rarily suspended recess privileges for two third-grade students who lodged a false allegation against their teacher. [21] Certainly, no record of the incident will be placed in the student file, because the Office of Civil Rights would consider that action equal to retribution. However, each allegation, factual or not, is recorded in the educator's file. Stu-dents hold great power in their hands—the power to end a career.

■■■■■■■■■■■■■■■■■■■■■■■■■■■■■■■■■■■■■■■

ARE TEACHERS EASY TARGETS?

The professional nature of teaching demands that educators under-stand and nurture students. Educators encourage intellectual and emotional discovery and they also expect students to make mistakes. Nonetheless, some mistakes are much more serious than others. Stu-dents may not understand the ramifications of a false allegation for a teacher's career. When a teacher is falsely accused of misconduct, more than one teacher's reputation is destroyed. Trust and confidence are also decimated for teachers, students, parents, and the greater community. Parker Palmer writes, "Teachers make an easy target, for they are such a common species and powerless to strike back. We blame teachers for being unable to cure social ills that no one knows how to treat; we insist that they instantly adopt whatever 'solution' has most recently been concocted by our national panacea machine; and in the process, we demoralize, even paralyze the very teachers who would help us find our way."[22] False allegations of misconduct can happen and do happen.

■■■■■■■■■■■■■■■■■■■■■■■■■■■■■■■■■■■■■■■

CAN A TEACHER BE PREPARED FOR A WRONGFUL ALLEGATION?

Is it possible to identify *potentially* dangerous situations? Can teachers be proactive? The actions taken by teachers in the first hours after they are aware of problematic behavior by students require quick decisions. What response is expected by parents, school administrators, and, perhaps more important, courts of law? Your response must be able to withstand legal, ethical, and professional scrutiny. The career of the educator is on the line should a case of alleged teacher sexual misconduct go to civil or criminal court.

Handling a false allegation of sexual misconduct is like playing with dynamite. Perhaps a false allegation of misconduct happens only once in a teacher's career. Unfortunately, once is enough to taint a flawless teaching record. Clearly, the classroom teacher has the most to lose. Knowing what to do about inappropriate, unwanted romantic student behavior will increase student safety, teacher success, and uphold school district credibility.

■■■

WHAT HAS HAPPENED TO YOU?

A dearth of research in this area needs to be corrected. If you have experienced a situation of false allegation of teacher misconduct, please complete the survey at the end of chapter 7. All accounts will be kept confidential.

■■■■■■■■■■■■■■■■■■■■■■■■■■■■■■■■■■■■■■■

NOTES

1. Perry Zirkel, "Abuse of Students or by Students?" *Phi Delta Kappan* 75 (December 1993): 344–46.

2. *In re Heather B.* Md. No.90, Sept. Term 2001, June 7, 2002.

3. Michael Gillis, "Sometimes Kids Falsely Accuse Teachers to Get Back at Them," *Chicago Sun-Times*, 20 April 1998, final edition.

4. *Peaster Independent School District v. Glodfelty*, Court of Appeals of Texas, Second District, Fort Worth 63 S.W. 3rd 1 2001: Tex. App. Lexis 3105.

5. American Association of University Women, "Hostile Hallways: The AAUW Survey on Sexual Harassment in America's Schools" (Washington, D.C.: American Association of University Women, 2001).

6. Metropolitan Life Insurance Company, "American Teacher, 1999: Violence in America's Public Schools: Five Years Later" (New York: Metropolitan Life Insurance Company, 1999).

7. Carol Shakeshaft and Audrey Cohan, "Sexual Abuse of Students by School Personnel," *Phi Delta Kappan* 76 (March 1995): 512–20.

8. Sally Beatty, "MTV Ratings Soar Off Gross Humor, Sex—and That's the Tame Stuff," *Wall Street Journal*, 20 April 2001.

9. Susan Ince, "A Woman Too Early: The Dangerous Trend Toward Early Puberty," *Redbook*, October 1998, 158–61.

10. Beth Ann Krier, "First-Graders Fighting Over Make-up? High Heels on the Playground? Some Say Young Girls Are on a Too Fast Track to Adulthood," *Los Angeles Times*, 15 January 1991, home edition.

11. Metropolitan Life Insurance Company, "American Teacher, 1999: Violence in America's Public Schools: Five Years Later" (New York: Metropolitan Life Insurance Company, 1999).

12. Ancel, Glink, Diamond, Bush, DiCianni, and Rolek, P.C. "Teacher/Sexual Harassment," *Education Law Report* No.1 (November 1998): 1–12.

13. Bureau of Justice Statistics, "National Crime Victimization Survey" (Washington, D.C.: U.S. Department of Justice, 2001).

14. Bernice Sandler, *Educator's Guide to Controlling Sexual Harassment* (Washington, D.C.: Thompson, 2001).

15. American Association of University Women, "Hostile Hallways: The AAUW Survey on Bullying, Teasing and Sexual Harassment in America's Schools" (Washington, D.C.: American Association of University Women 2001).

16. Valerie Lee, Robert Croninger, Eleanor Linn, and Xianglei Chen, "The Culture of Sexual Harassment in Secondary Schools," *American Educational Research Journal* 33 (Summer 1996): 338–417.

17. Ann Schwab, "The Sweep of Sexual Harassment," *Cornell Law Review* 86 (March 2001): 548.

18. Susan Strauss, *Sexual Harassment and Teens* (Minneapolis, MN: Free Spirit, 1992).

19. *Stoneking v. Bradford Area School District*, United States Court of Appeals for the Third Circuit, 882 F. 2nd 720; 1989 App. Lexis 15711.

20. *In re Heather B.* Md. No. 90, Sept. Term 2001, June 7, 2002.

21. "Fourth-Grade Girls Are Fined $5.00 Each for Sex-Abuse Hoax," *St. Louis Post Dispatch*, 9 May 1998, Five Star Lift Edition.

22. Parker Palmer, *The Courage to Teach* (San Francisco: Jossey-Bass, 1998).

CHAPTER 2

"LOLITA" IN THE CLASSROOM

OVERVIEW

Who is Lolita? What impact will she (or he) have upon your teaching career?

Several questions provide the focus for this inquiry. How can teachers identify inappropriate behavior? Are certain students at greater risk of inappropriate behavior? What legal issues are involved when students seek special attention from their classroom instructors? This chapter will provide a working definition of the *Lolita* complex, indicative behavior, and danger signs. Additionally, school-sponsored activities and locations that could prove troublesome will be described. Finally, a brief case study drawn from the classroom is presented to promote discussion and reflection by the reader.

OBJECTIVES

After completing this chapter, the reader should be able to:

1. Describe behavior signs of problematic sexual behavior in elementary and secondary youth.

2. Define S.A.C.Y.
3. Describe quid pro quo environments.

■■

IMPORTANT TERMS

confidentiality: Family Education Rights and Privacy Act of 1974 restricts access to a student's records to certain parties.

grooming behavior: engagement strategies; here harassers gain the special trust of the victim, or take advantage of special relationships that already exist.

ideation: the forming of ideas; fantasies.

Lolita: a fictional character; a child who exhibits seductive behavior toward an adult.

quid pro quo: a relationship in which something is given or withheld in exchange for something else (sexual behavior).

rape: forced sexual intercourse, including psychological coercion as well as physical force.

sexual assault: a wide range of victimizations; includes grabbing, fondling, verbal threats.

sexual battery: an incident that includes rape, fondling, indecent liberties.

Sexually Abusive (Aggressive) Children and Youth (S.A.C.Y.): children who exhibit sexually problematic behavior. When confronted, children engaging in sexually aggressive behavior typically blame the behavior on others or angrily deny their behavior.

transference: when students in need of emotional support adopt feelings for their teachers that are similar to the feelings they have had in a past close relationship, such as for a parent.

■■

WHO IS LOLITA?

The *Lolita* complex (in common usage) is an unfounded romantic attachment to an authority figure and is based on the title character from the 1958 novel by Vladimir Vladimirovich Nabokov.[1] The character, a precocious teenager, seemed to possess mature sexual understanding, and actively sought the attentions of older men. The novel shocked the American reading public and provided the title for a troubling complex of behaviors exhibited by children or teenage youth. The *Lolita* complex describes students, *male or female*, who seek to feel wanted, favored, or needed by an adult, and who express their needs via sexual messages and seductive behavior.[2] Daily classroom interactions provide opportunity for students who *intend* to cross the boundaries of traditional professional teacher–student relationships.

Although *Lolita* has been around since 1958, the effect of a "crush" on the teacher is a perennial occurrence in the classroom. Crushes are a very normal part of growing up. Teachers, coaches, and other school personnel in daily contact with students often become mentors and friends to their students.[3] Consequently, teachers may serve as parental substitutes or the object of romantic fantasies by their students. Students often see the adult as attractive, perfect, and self-assured, all things they do not feel about themselves.[4]

Beyond daydreams, some students may actively seek special attention from an accepting, experienced adult in the classroom environment.[5] A feeling of affection toward a teacher may shift to become a dangerous need for sole attention from a targeted adult.[6]

Educators are public figures who hold a unique position of trust and authority. The mere hint of sexual misconduct may have a devastating effect on a teacher's career. Such a stigma can result in the loss of employment (even if the teacher is officially cleared of all charges). In fact, teachers are held to a higher standard by state, judicial, and community members because they enjoy the "special privilege" to shelter and educate our most vulnerable citizens.[7]

Schools are not separate from modern society, nor are they asexual environments. Children may experience rich fantasies about adult educational personnel. Effective teachers watch for patterns of behavior in their students, patterns that may indicate troubling attitudes and emotions. Current scrutiny by the public demands that classroom teachers increase awareness, sensitivity, and response to inappropriate student behavior. For example:

> In English class, right in front of the teacher, Joey will say, "I think I'm getting hard" when his girlfriend walks in or if he wants to embarrass some girls.[8]

A group of third-graders uses force to hold down a female class-mate on the playground while one of them climbs on top of her and pretends to have sexual intercourse with her.

A fifth-grade boy repeatedly attempts to touch a classmate's chest and genital area and rub against her. He constantly asks her for sex.[9]

■■■

WHO ARE S.A.C.Y. CHILDREN?

In the past ten years, quite a tragedy has taken place. Youth offend-ers, often as young as ten years old, perpetrate sexual predatory acts. Juvenile justice and child protection services report that arrests for children less than 12 years old have increased 125 percent for gen-eral sex offenses and 190 percent for forcible rape.[10] Sadly, children who commit sexual assaults, rapes, and molestation on other small children are undoubtedly sex abuse victims themselves. The juvenile court system simply has no incarceration plan for such criminals.

Such children are often designated "Sexually Abusive Children and Youth" and placed in court-mandated, therapeutic situations. These children are provided intensive therapeutic services and returned to family settings. School is a part their therapy because it offers a chance for a normalized life. Although they are restricted from other children without constant adult supervision, S.A.C.Y. (pronounced *say-see*) children interact with teachers and peers on a daily basis. Teach-ers who have students with S.A.C.Y. plans may not be aware of their special needs. Federal mandates in the Family Educational Rights and Privacy Act of 1974 restrict open access to permanent records. Privacy issues require school officials to be extremely cautious when releas-ing information regarding the S.A.C.Y. individual education plan with-out prior parental consent.[11]

Sexually aggressive children usually exhibit the following be-haviors:

1. They *respond sexually* to nonsexual behavior conditions. Classroom examples would include hugging a child, fixing a hair barrette, compliments, pats on the back, physical prox-imity of another, or holding a hand.

2. They *select targets* they find desirable.

3. They *assess how much risk* is present.

4. They *perpetuate the abuse*.

5. They *protect themselves* from discovery.

6. They find ways to *excuse themselves* from the abuse. They blame others or deny their actions.

Regardless of setting, recidivism rates continue to be quite high for S.AC.Y. children.[12]

■■

WHAT IS GROOMING BEHAVIOR?

A symptom of grooming behavior, an acute conduct disorder, is the systematic preparation of victims. The term "grooming" is used in the sense of preparation for an event. Sexual abusers begin their crimes by establishing an atmosphere of trust with the intended victim. Gifts, favors, and compliments form the basis for this grooming relationship. Unfortunately, the relationship is, in reality, intended to be reciprocal. The generous behavior of the perpetrator is to be rewarded. The victim is expected to give sexual favors for the attention granted by the abuser. Grooming behavior can take place *within* the confines of the classroom. Students who consistently bring little gifts, stay after class to do favors, and seek out opportunities to compliment teachers may be seeking inappropriate relationships with teaching mentors.[13]

■■■

WHAT OTHER PROBLEMATIC BEHAVIORS MIGHT BE SEEN?

Students can exhibit problematic behaviors whether or not they are identified as S.AC.Y. Children need attention and the desire for attention may escalate to allegations of sexual misconduct. Teachers must be diligent and recognize danger signs. Mental disorders are not as readily apparent in children as they are in adults. Often undiagnosed mental illness will be present in elementary and middle school youth.

Problematic behaviors by students in regard to false accusations of teacher sexual misconduct would include:

1. Controlling behaviors
2. Repeated lying
3. Delusion and ideation
4. Attention-seeking
5. Seductive behavior
6. A grand sense of self-importance
7. Expectations of special favors
8. Surprise that the teacher likes and admires them
9. Poor relationships with peers
10. Taking advantage of others to indulge their own desires
11. Rich, fantastic daydreams
12. Inability to see long-term consequences of their action[14]

Needy or traumatized students often grant their teachers the same emotional privileges (e.g., holding hands, placing arms around the teacher, leaning against the teacher, playing with teacher's hair, touching teacher's clothing) as romantic suitors. This transference, from teacher to close friend, signals dangerous waters for teaching professionals.[15]

Disciplinary restrictions in the classroom may be unwelcome by children who are experts in dodging a punishment. Children in state foster-home placements are schooled in what constitutes reasons for a change in placement. Allegations of sexual abuse provide a fast ticket out of a situation that may be too restrictive for a child's taste.[16]

Serious disruption in a student's life due to traumatic life events can cause a sense that the student is being overwhelmed by stress and may increase overt control behaviors. Although teachers may provide strong support for students in crisis, potential romantic interests for favored teachers may simultaneously intensify. Students as well as adults exhibit a greater vulnerability during times of life crises. Such life events might include:

1. Death of a parent
2. Sibling leaving home

3. Family separation
4. Family remarriage
5. Divorce
6. Personal injury
7. Death of a close friend
8. Beginning or ending of school
9. Suffering verbal or physical abuse at home
10. Pregnancy
11. Change in financial status of the family
12. A brush with the law
13. Clinical depression
14. Change in residence
15. Loss of a job
16. Loss of a peer love relationship[17]

The last group of students who would falsely report teacher sexual misconduct is those students who have issues of revenge or who seek monetary gain.

Experienced teachers know that the above indicators could describe just about any child at different times of the school year. The student who poses the greatest danger of making a false allegation of teacher misconduct is a potent mix of many indicators. Great effort is required to consistently maintain a fabricated story of sexual victimization, but for students who seek attention, it is worth the payoff.

■■

HOW WILL YOU IDENTIFY A *LOLITA* COMPLEX?

The students like you. They think you are the greatest teacher ever. You try to be a parent, mentor, and teacher all rolled into one package. This is the primary reason you went into teaching. Unfortunately, the admiration you inspire often provides the basis for an unwarranted romantic attachment that defines a *Lolita* complex.

Questionable student behavior usually has clear warning signs. Knowing those signs will alert the teacher to intervene, redirect youthful energies, and provide a safe, nonhostile classroom environment. As you read the following, keep the following two ideas in mind. First, many of these behaviors are considered sexual harassment.[18] Second, many behaviors will appear as common events in a fast-paced classroom. In fact, the behaviors are quite common, but added together they signal a dangerous liability situation for the teacher.

Students seeking special attention from a teacher may

1. write notes that express a heightened affection for the teacher;
2. make jokes about sexual topics within the teacher's hearing;
3. use double entendre or innuendo when asking questions;
4. start rumors about sexual favors or trysts with the teacher;
5. call the teacher's home phone or cell phone, perhaps just to hang up;
6. exhibit "grooming" behavior to establish a quid pro quo relationship.

All behaviors need not be present to signal a troublesome situation. Teachers cannot afford to ignore troublesome student behavior. Even small incidents may be reported in a judicial hearing considering evidence as to whether a teacher took advantage of his or her position to *encourage* highly impressionable students.[19]

■■■

NOTES ARE JUST NOTES, AREN'T THEY?

Student-to-student notes are a perennial occurrence in the American classroom. In fact, many teachers wish students would spend equal time on their homework as on their elaborate note-writing and note-folding rituals. Students from elementary through high school delight in writing and passing notes. When students want to express a crush on the teacher, a note, a nonconfrontational communication, often seems the easiest way to go.

Imagine the teacher's reaction when he received the following invitation from a third-grade student:

Dear Mr. G,
I invite you to my class play—room 38. I have a crush on you. I am your dream. I invite you to my house. . . . I am 10 years old in

3rd grade. I want to get naked with you. My phone number is ... Call; I am sexy as can be, call me.

> Your Friend,
> Victoria

Or imagine the second-grade teacher who received the following two notes, one day apart.

Dear Miss N.,
I like you, Miss N. I love you. You are the best teacher in the whole world. You are nice to me.

Dear Miss N.,
I love you very much. I wanted to tell you about it. I am glad you love me too. I like you for a girlfriend. You are there for me. I have a ring for you. I will bring it tomorrow. I can't wait. What is your phone number?

Finally, a sixth-grade student gave a demonstration speech on "How to Be a Player" and used his teacher's first name when describing how to procure a personal phone number from a girl.

The first thing you do when you see a fine girl is you approach her with determination. You do a breath check to see if it is not good. When you are finally in front of her you then say, "Hey Robin, do you have a man?" Now, you do one of two things. If she says yes, you leave her alone, because her man is somewhere around. If she says no, you say, "Well, can I have your number?" Then give her "the look" when you lick your lips.

The speech was given to the delight of the other students and the chagrin of the teacher, who had not previewed the script. The message was clear; the student was out of line; the teacher was embarrassed, but what could she do?

At first thought, a teacher accepts these notes as simple tokens of affection, written with harmless intent. A more astute evaluation will serve to warn teachers that the notes reveal more than harmless intent. In each case, the student is expressing thoughts above the maturity level of most primary students. Taken in context, the student is suggesting inappropriate conduct and contact (e.g., phone calls and house visits, personal gifts). Taken out of context, the student seems to be implying teacher encouragement of the romantic overtures. Occasionally, the notes contain crude drawings depicting sexual scenes. Such drawings may be symptoms of abnormal psychosocial development. Teachers have the professional responsibility to refer such students to the care of a qualified school counselor. Unfortunately, due to the ages of the students, elementary teachers might dismiss the notes as unimportant. All notes expressing such thoughts are crucial artifacts if the child chooses to progress in his or her fantasy. Additionally, each *original* note or drawing should be retained, dated, and include anecdotal notations. Remember, such written evidence is extremely valuable during parent conferences, district policy hearings, or court litigation.

■■■

WHAT DO YOU THINK OF THIS PICTURE?

Middle and secondary school students delight in hearing what teachers think about their youth culture celebrities. Students may show pictures of semi-clad models to peers and teachers. Locker decorations often include teenage idols in provocative attire. Students who seek a teacher's opinion in regard to these pictures do so simply to broach the subject with the teacher. Leaving sex-related objects on the teacher's desk or in open classroom areas, sure to be noticed by the teacher, may also be a ploy to attract attention and turn the subject toward sex. A middle school teacher, who found a used condom in her teacher's text, was asked, "What do you think of page 32?" by several seventh-grade male students. This type of harassment is not limited to women teachers. Male teachers just as easily can be the targets of off-color jokes from male or female students.[20] Teachers' reactions must be above reproach by parents and school administrators. Be careful what you say. Even off-the-cuff comments will be reported, perhaps out of context.

■■■

HOW CAN YOU TELL IF STUDENTS ARE JUST JOKING?

The classroom is a milieu of verbal directions, interactions, and instruction. It is a kingdom of words. Silly, inappropriate student comments are commonplace. Nonetheless, double entendre is less common and easily identified. Double entendre, or "two intents," refers to the denotation and connotation of student remarks. One meaning usually has an immoral message. The best litmus test for double-meaning comments employs the same standard used to evaluate sexual harassment situations. If the comment makes the listener uncomfortable, or seems to carry sexual messages, it is inappropriate. Middle and secondary school students are quite adept in interpersonal communication and the use of language, and therefore may craft double comments such as: "Sure, I'll stay after class, if *you ask!*" "Can I help you in *any way?*" "I need some help with my *homework.*" "Are you interested *in this?*" If the comment or the *intent* makes you uncomfortable, you must tell the student. Teachers don't help the student by laughing. In fact, you will be rewarding inappropriate behavior. Far worse, you are "establishing an environment favorable to assault behavior." Sexual harassment legal standards require teachers to clearly tell offenders that they don't like the comment or the tone and not to repeat the behavior. According to the Office of Civil Rights, sexual harassment can involve verbal or physical conduct of a sexual nature.[21] Your immediate response to the inappropriate comments must send a clear message that such comments will not be tolerated. Failure to identify inappropriate behavior allows the problem to continue and, often, to escalate.

■■

COULD I LOSE MY JOB BECAUSE OF A RUMOR?

A final form of inappropriate student comment holds the most potential to damage a career: private comments from one student to another. The mere whispered expression of an imagined sexual liaison with a teaching professional may become the payoff for an attention-starved student. Student comments are potent messages. They may mention teacher favoritism, spawn rumors, or elaborate on fantasies about teacher-student relationships. Certainly half-truths and misunderstanding abound. If overheard by other school personnel or parents, student comments about a teacher's behavior *must* be reported to child protective agencies as allegations of misconduct. For example, if a student gossips that a teacher has invited another student to a romantic tryst, that report is valid cause to initiate a full investigation by child protective services. The mere hint of sexual misconduct by an educator is enough to begin a criminal investigation, even if the reporting student is not a credible witness. Parents, police, child protection services, school administrators, and the media may vigorously pursue an investigation based on the flimsiest rumor.

Rumors attract attention. Rumors have four characteristics that facilitate transition. They are:

1. The importance of the subject: Teachers are important elements in the school setting and therefore the child's world. The popularity of the teacher only escalates the speed of the rumor.

2. Ambiguity of the current situation: Details to support the student's contention of a teacher–student liaison may be fabricated by student and friends. Attention-seeking behavior begins exponential growth of stories and reports.

3. Personal anxiety: The "What if this is true?" tone begins to permeate even slight "hearsay" evidence.

4. General uncertainty as to resolution.[22] Fantastic imaginings about how this situation might end.

Such a rumor guarantees immediate reaction in the school and greater community. A rumor often *will* be taken as a true disclosure.

■■■

DO STUDENTS KNOW THE CONSEQUENCES OF THE LIE?

Most students simply do not know the serious consequences of their actions; in other cases they do not care. Erik Erikson describes adolescence as a time of "as if"—a time of experimentation in various adult roles and ideation of fantasies. Adolescents in this period of development do not see themselves as being held fully responsible for mistakes they make as they try on new roles.[23] Unfortunately, ideation can become coercive in nature. Coercive, narcissistic students seek power over others through raw humor, lying, or aggression and quickly learn how to get their way. Coercive students lose sight of the long-term implications of what they say and continue to be rewarded by short-term benefits.[24]

WHY CAN'T STUDENTS CALL MY HOME?

Students may call the teacher's home phone or cell phone, perhaps just to hang up. Thanks to modem technology, many teachers have caller ID, which provides a phone number read-out indicating the origin of the call and is especially helpful when prank callers interrupt the night hours. Nonetheless, students may call your home under the guise of homework questions. Personal comments abound during phone calls between teacher and student. They provide dangerous and fertile ground for misinterpretation or conjecture. Keeping precise notes of phone conversations between teachers and students may help recall the time, duration, and subject of each call. You should not rely on your memory. Write down essential information. Your professional notes are considered valid evidence in legal investigations.

WHAT IS A QUID PRO QUO RELATIONSHIP?

A quid pro quo relationship is defined as something given or withheld in exchange for something else.[25] "Grooming" is the most troubling of all characteristics of deviant student behavior. Teachers who do not know the warning signs of sexual aggressors may interpret grooming behavior as indicative of student affection, but there is an undercurrent of sexual expectation that colors student intent. Used in context with the *Lolita* complex, a student will attempt to excel, volunteer, or show favors to teachers in exchange for special attention from them.

WHAT ARE THE MOST DANGEROUS SETTINGS FOR TEACHERS?

A review of civil court cases involving alleged teacher sexual misconduct uncovers a pattern of circumstances and settings. Locations and activities that increase opportunities for students to concoct stories of inappropriate teacher behavior include:

1. Field trips: When groups of students are separated during a field trip, teachers are at greater risk of being alone with a small group. Don't be fooled into thinking that two students will be enough to guarantee a witness who would substantiate teacher innocence. In several court cases, groups of students backed each other's fraudulent stories.

2. Transporting students in private vehicles: Beyond the insurance liability, placing a student in the teacher's private vehicle instantly provides an opportunity for the student to charge you with misconduct. Driving instructors need to be very aware that being alone with one student in a car is inadvisable.

3. Invitation to family residence: Students should never be invited to a teacher's home. If teachers wish to have a party, select a public place such as a restaurant and invite several responsible adults to help with supervision.

4. Classroom seclusion: Most schools were not built for open sight lines. The task of the teacher to be seen at all times is a difficult one. Do not cover the window of the classroom; students have used this practice to allege lunchtime and conference period trysts. Never have students in the classroom without other adults in the area. If a student is ill or working on homework, find space in the library, clinic, or front office for him or her to sit. You must not provide an opportunity for students to be in a secluded area with you. Walking a fine line to keep out of secluded areas is well worth a little extra planning.

5. Extracurricular activities: From football games to speech contests, teachers spend hours after school and on weekends doing their jobs. It is no wonder that the largest group of teachers accused of sexual misconduct is extracurricular and electives teachers.[26] Music directors, cheerleading sponsors, drama directors, and athletic coaches are most at risk for a wrongful allegation. The scenarios are too numerous to give specific directions of safety; however, a general rule applies— Think Ahead. The case law is clear; *in education the perception is the reality.*

A charge of teacher sexual misconduct is considered quite improbable to most teachers. That is, until it happens to them. The simple truth is that such a charge rarely comes out of "nowhere." Many situations can be anticipated and avoided by prudent educators. Yet, when a school district or teacher association attorney proffers clear warnings for teachers to stay out of isolated situations or to refrain from touching students, they are met with scoffing from the faculty. Why? The closeness of the student-teacher relationship engenders hugs, pats on the back, and frequent physical contact. The sad fact is that teachers may be the only adults the students have on their side emotionally. Imposing a cool distance between teachers and students flies in the face of the image of a dedicated, caring teacher. In short, warnings of perceived misconduct are either absent or go unheeded by all but the wisest teachers.

Student teachers rarely know the Title IX definition of sexual harassment. In a recent survey conducted with over 100 student teachers, only one student felt confident regarding the identification of sexual harassment according to the Title IX guidelines. This student, previously a military service member, was required to attend training sessions for the identification of sexually harassing behavior as a part of his military service. One knowledgeable person in a hundred respondents! This informal survey paints a bleak picture for school administrators who assume student teachers will follow school policy regarding the prohibition of sexually harassing behavior. It follows that student teachers who fail to police their own behavior will also fail to correct potentially dangerous situations between students. The reality is that at no juncture in their professional preparation do most student teachers receive adequate training in recognizing and controlling sexually harassing behavior in the classroom.

Dangerous behavior patterns, perhaps learned from four years of college social interactions, and the fact that student teachers may be very close in age to their classroom students set the stage for tragedy. High school and middle school students attempt to affiliate themselves with young student teachers, perceived to be attractive, successful, and powerful. Many student teachers are barely four years older than their classroom charges. The closeness in age encourages sexual comments and behaviors by students toward their student teachers. In fact, women teachers and younger or less-experienced teachers are often targets for student verbal and/or sexual abuse. Certainly, sexual harassment legislation mandates quick and decisive action by school administrators to end verbal abuse with sexual overtones. Unfortunately, the building principal is often the last to know or intervene in questionable student-teacher performance.

New legal expectations for practicing classroom educators are not commonly covered in teacher education texts or in preprofessional field practicum. Student teachers receive little instruction in public school law and therefore could not describe simple legal parameters regarding liability, negligence, harassment, or professional ethics. They are, in most cases, wholly unprepared to identify sexual-harassing student behavior or to exhibit acceptable teacher behavior. Another caveat to this lack of explicit preparation is that student teachers often seek to emulate mentors.

Unfortunately, experienced classroom teachers often hold misunderstandings regarding sexually harassing behavior by students. In fact, most university professors lack training in Title IX guidelines for public school settings. Unbelievably, many problematic student teacher behaviors are accepted and/or encouraged by cooperating teachers and university professors, who misinterpret the behavior as a form of friendliness toward students.

Student teachers simply do not have opportunities to practice identification of sexually harassing behaviors or effective classroom intervention strategies. Student teachers need adequate time and expert guidance to process and *un*learn behaviors they may consider correct but in reality are clear violations of Title IX. For example, in *Doe v. Berkley County School District*, a student teacher offered to take a female high school student for a "ride in his car." Although the building principal enlightened the student teacher regarding the inappropriate comments, no record of the incident was given to the university supervisor (who rated the student as excellent in the teaching placement). One year later, now a substitute for the same district, the young man was involved in sexual behavior with two female high school students. One wonders, had the correct action been taken at the first sign of his poor decision making, if the young man would ever have had a career in teaching. Unfortunately, not understanding that certain behaviors are sexually harassing will not absolve the student (or school district) from legal, moral, or ethical responsibility. Student teachers need the support of informed instructors to identify and assess problematic behaviors.

Experienced teachers as well as first-year and student teachers must begin to see the following actions for what they are—foolish, cavalier behaviors that may end a teaching career in total, shame-filled failure. Each behavior in the following list comes directly from a court case regarding teacher sexual misconduct. Readers should measure their own professional practice against the identified behaviors to avoid. Remember, you only need one case of questionable decision making to place your career in jeopardy.

What situations must teachers, or anyone dealing with young people, seek to avoid?

1. *Do not tease with flirting overtones.* Kids like it when you tease them. They understand that you are kidding in good-natured fun. Not true. Ask yourself, if taken out of context, could your words stand on their own merit? You can be certain your comments *will* be taken out of context. Title IX guidelines of sexual harassment clearly delineate limits to humor. The same comment you think is quite funny may send a completely different message to the listener. Any potential jurist will be instructed to consider the perception of the victim over the intent of the perpetrator. Simply said, don't joke in a sexual or flirtatious manner with students or faculty members. Students just may take you seriously, and faculty members will remember that off-the-cuff comment. Be careful what you say in the classroom and faculty lounge and during extracurricular activities. Your words may return cast in a much different light than first spoken.

2. *Never be alone in the classroom with a student.* When you direct a student to return to the classroom to finish an assignment, you must include several students in the grouping or arrange for a neutral location. Classrooms have restricted sight lines; just leaving the door to the hallway open will not serve the purpose of ensuring a credible witness for the teacher. Teachers must set up a situation where there is another *responsible* party to neutralize any rumor. If that is impossible or poses great inconvenience, perhaps the student could finish the assignment in a counseling room, a library, the principal's office, or another classroom where class is continuing.

3. *Stay out of isolated situations after school–for your own safety.* Don't stay in the classroom alone after school dismissal. Should a student return, it would be difficult to keep the

atmosphere above suspicion. Close and lock the door to your classroom. Post a sign that reads "I'll Be Right Back." Students in a hurry will not stay. Other students may wait for a few minutes, and then leave you a note in return. Simply said, do not allow entry by a single student—just don't answer the door. You might also work after school in the teacher's lounge, library, or computer room.

4. *Avoid expressions of physical affection.* Several teacher associations have provided a list of appropriate physical gestures. Past "approved" contacts have included touching the upper arm, a pat on the back, shaking hands, or an arm around the shoulder. Because this constraint seems too surgical for teachers, they simply ignore the advice. In fact, current court cases prove there simply is no "approved" physical contact appropriate in all settings between student and teacher. The best advice is to only touch students in a neutral manner and in the presence of other credible adults. Any other action is folly. Teachers have faced court testimony of student complaints that describe suspect physical conduct such as "a boyfriend-type hug," "patted my back, over my bra strap," "held my hand," "put her arm around my waist," "patted my hips," "hugged me too long," "patted my head," "bumped into me," and "gave me a backrub." Any teacher with more than a few months in the classroom could attest to the benign presence of such daily events. On the other hand, the end result of such physical demonstrations of affection may be that you will be expected to explain such actions in court. Explaining that you show such physical demonstrations to all students will only make matters worse. You never know what a simple hug is communicating to a student. You may be thinking "positive support." The student may be thinking "returned affection." Worse yet, for the student who has endured past physical or sexual abuse, such physical demonstrations bring terrible memories. In the face of such misunderstanding and potential for harm, why not curb your own behavior?

5. *Do not place yourself in an automobile alone with students.* You should not transport students in your own vehicle, simply for liability reasons. Furthermore, you should not get in

a student's car for a quick run to the local store. Any time you are in an isolated situation, you have spawned a "he said-she said" situation. Should you stop to get gasoline and perhaps purchase snacks for the student, you now have an eyewitness that you were purchasing treats for a child. If you follow that with any prolonged isolation or a time gap in travel, you have situation tailor-made for an allegation of sexual misconduct.

6. *Do not give out your home or cell phone number to students.* This is perhaps the most common mistake made by first-year teachers. Inexperienced teachers want to show students the best of intentions and a real-world concern for student achievement. Their phone number, home or cell, provides an avenue for questions or student concerns. In reality, phone conversations have great leeway to become opportunities for personal messages. Calls may have many listeners. Teachers who allow phone calls to their home or cell phone provide enterprising students with an opportunity for risky personal communication.

7. *Do not give out your personal e-mail address.* Students of all ages feel very comfortable with technology. Many know that instant messaging facilitates e-mail interruption, as long as the targeted person is online. Teachers find they cannot use their computer without constant obscene messages from multiple anonymous sources. Expecting law enforcement to track down the culprit is a pipe dream; expecting parents to curb computer privileges may be as elusive.

8. *Do not give presents to students.* When teachers hand out jewelry, T-shirts, cards, or personal notes, they find it difficult to explain in court. Juries wonder, why would a teacher favor a specific student with a gift unless something was expected in return? State boards of education and civil courts see this as quid pro quo, something given for a favor in return. Playing favorites with gifts encourages students to expect a special level of personal influence with the teacher.

9. *Do not attend social events held by students.* Family events such as graduations, weddings, and birthday parties are wonderful events to share with your students, but be wary they are not student-only celebrations. Should you arrive to

find all participants are underage, you must leave immediately. Attending a party given by students sets the scene for rampant rumors of inappropriate teacher actions.

10. *Do not invite students to your home.* Year-end parties and/or sleepovers offer students a view of teachers' personal lives. Remember, everything that happens in your domicile is your responsibility and may in fact become the basis for an allegation of sexual misconduct. Should you employ a student to baby-sit in your home, be sure there are plenty of safeguards for returning the student home. At no time should you be alone with the student.

11. *Do not lend money to students.* Every teacher has at some time lent lunch money to hungry students. Often teachers do not expect repayment; unfortunately, some have been repaid with the allegation that they gave the money to students to purchase special favors from them.

12. *Do not write personal notes to students.* Please remember, comments on graded papers are not covered in this advice. Personal letters to students are forbidden. What reason could a teacher have to begin and continue a personal correspondence outside of class? Parents and community will think the worst.

13. *Do not post student pictures in your room with suggestive titles or captions.* Labeling a student the "Cutest Girl in Town" or "My Special Girls" will mislead every student in your class. If you enjoy posting student pictures, do so without captions.

14. *Don't allow student to call you "Mom" or "Dad."* Although the title may be a result of true affection, the ability to use a nickname for you encourages students to step over the professional barrier that must be present in every classroom.

15. *School bus seating should be adult with adult.* Many allegations of teacher sexual misconduct have been fueled by a situation where an adult sat in a close-quarters bus seat with a student. Students in the rear of the bus rarely misbehave when two adults are sitting in adjacent seats. But should there be only one adult on the bus, he or she must take an entire seat exclusively.

16. *Do not take a student home from school.* Taking a student home poses its own problems. How do you know the house

is actually the student's residence? How do you know the house is safe for the student? Who is home to receive the student? Is there any potential for an assault on you? A verbal approval from a parent via phone to transport the student is not legal permission. How do you know the caller is the parent? You must call the local police to take the student home. This action may seem hard-hearted, but it is the only legal action you can take to ensure student safety (and your continued employment). The police will safely escort the student to the door. They will confirm this is the correct residence and inquire if there is a responsible party to supervise the student.

17. *Be aware that field trips that include an overnight stay pose problematic situations.* Entering a hotel or motel room where students are housed is also not a good idea. Teams of teachers or certified personnel, rather than a single person, should supervise students during extended field trips, especially when checking rooms. Lock-ins in any setting pose a dangerous risk for teachers who may be in the wrong place at the wrong time. Prior planning for staffing must include male and female instructors. Male teachers dealing with female students quickly experience a double standard in education. Female teachers seem to have more leeway in supervision of all students than male teachers. Perhaps based on the maternal role, female teachers may supervise girls and boys in a gender-neutral manner.

18. *Do not date a student, even a former student.* Remember that sexual abuse of minors has no statute of limitations in many states. Several court cases have been initiated 10 to 30 years after the alleged event. A minor can never legally give consent for a sexual relationship.

19. *Don't give a student an extended hall pass to move freely around the building.* Writing out semester-long passes encourages students to feel they have a special relationship with you. They also feel a bit more important than their peers because they share your attention and trust. That semester-long hall pass could equally appear as a ticket to a tryst. Take the time to write out a specific pass for a specific day and time and note the reason. You may need the notation to prompt your memory in case of an allegation. Collect and keep all expired hall passes.

20. *Mentoring relationships must maintain professional boundaries.* When school districts formally pair teachers with at-risk children, the potential exists for eroding professional barriers. The practice of getting to know students and their families is a good idea, but taking students into your personal life is a bad idea. When establishing a mentoring relationship, teachers are expected to keep a positive, supporting relationship that is clearly aboveboard, on a professional standing, and beyond reproach.

21. *Always have all students due to arrive and depart at the same time.* Extracurricular activities often take place in an empty school. When a single student arrives early or stays after others are gone, the odds improve that an allegation of misconduct will be made.

22. *Save all student notes.* Although you should never read a student note out loud in the classroom, you should never throw away any student-to-student notes. The best practice is to read the note and document the date and the student's name. Keep the note until the end of the year.

23. *Do not post cartoons that could appear sexist or demeaning.* The times have changed. Posting notes that ridicule males or females sets a negative tone in the classroom and encourages students to mimic such behavior.

24. *Do not allow students to call you by your first name.* No matter how informal the setting, you must keep a professional distance from your students. When students attempt to call you any other name, correct them immediately.

25. *When planning any off-campus activity, include male and female supervisors.* Even if you invite a very dependable parent, you will need to ensure that females supervise girls and males supervise boys.

26. *Do not allow inappropriate joking between students.* Federal mandates restrict public comments in a sexually harassing tone. Regardless of whether you join in the conservation, you are responsible to immediately stop sexual joking, flirting, or actions. Use your leadership to immediately stop the situation. Your silence in such a situation implies your consent.

27. *Do not share information about one student with another.* Maintaining confidentiality is of the utmost importance.

28. *Do not make a professional referral to a clinical counselor or physician without the parents' or legal guardian's approval.* The parent or legal guardian is the only legal entity to approve medical or psychiatric care for a minor.

Be forewarned: Each behavior holds the potential for danger. If you think that only high school teachers need to be wary, you are wrong. Even third-graders have leveled false sexual abuse charges against their teachers. And worse, when charges were recanted, no punishment more serious than missing a few outdoor recesses was meted out.

Effective teachers follow clearly outlined plans of professional behavior. The next chapter will help teachers plan effective ways to correct student behavior that crosses the line of appropriate professional teacher–student relationships.

■■■

CASE STUDIES

The following case studies are provided to encourage discussion. The characters and situations are purely fictional.

1. A high school English teacher is working at her desk after school. A freshman student who has returned to school to speak to her approaches. The teacher feels isolated in the room at the end of a long hallway, and during the conversation she continues to move toward the communication button on the wall. Before she can reach the button, the student exposes himself. The teacher calls for help and runs for the door. The student catches her and leans against her, pinning her to the wall. She manages to push him away and escape to the hallway. The teacher runs to the front office. She returns with an office secretary to find the student has vacated the room. The teacher talks to the high school principal, who promises to deal with the situation, but the next day the student is again present in her English class as if nothing had happened. When the teacher demands an answer from the school administration as to why no disciplinary action has been taken with the student, she is told he is the son of a high-ranking district employee. The next day, the teacher files

sexual assault charges against the student with the local police, only to be told by school personnel that she enticed the
student and that she has been placed on disciplinary leave
without pay. The teacher loses her job for immoral behavior.
No action is ever taken against the boy.

2. A football coach has been assigned at-risk students to mentor toward graduation. One student, a girl, volunteers to help
with football equipment and keep team stats. The girl tells the
coach about her drug experimentation and abusive family. Sitting in the coach's office, she often likes to rub his shoulders.
Love notes and gifts begin to appear on the coach's desk. The
girl gives him her school picture and writes on the reverse,
"You are more than a dad to me." The coach continues to
welcome her visits to the coaching office and provides hallway passes for her to come at any time of the school day. He
also writes notes back to the girl telling her how much she
means to him. The girl's mother accuses the coach of sexual
misconduct after she finds the love notes. The coach retires
quickly, and the girl spends time in a treatment facility due to
chronic depression and attempted suicide.

3. A science teacher seeks volunteer lab assistants. The assistants
work together to set up lab experiments and to restock equipment and supplies. Two female students work as a team during their off hours. On one day, one student is absent and
the other appears to work in the lab. The following day this
student shares a story of having sexual intercourse with the
science teacher in the school lab during the lunch hour. Both
students now begin to add details to the story until a high
school counselor overhears them. The counselor reports the
story to the principal. The teacher is handcuffed and arrested
at the classroom door. The teacher is suspended until police,
child welfare authorities, and the school district can investigate. The teacher successfully passes a polygraph test with
local police. While the school investigation is ongoing, all students who have this teacher are called into the office to offer
information regarding his in-class behavior and comments toward female students. The teacher resigns his teaching position during the school district investigation. Six weeks later,
the girls recant their story, claiming their motivation was that
"We thought he was cute." No disciplinary action is taken

against the girls. They continue to keep the teacher's school yearbook picture posted in their lockers.

Discussion Questions

- In each case, there are warning signs. What are they?
- What pre-allegation circumstances could have been changed to ensure a better outcome for the educator?
- In each case, the school district acted in accordance with the law. Do you agree with the actions? Why or why not?
- Why would teachers opt to resign if they know they are innocent of the charges?

■■

NOTES

1. V. Vladimirovich Nabokov, *Lolita* (New York: Putnam, 1958).

2. American Psychiatric Association, *Diagnostic and Statistical Manual of Mental Disorders*, 4th ed. (Washington, D.C.: American Psychiatric Association, 2000).

3. William Fibkins, "Preventing Teacher Sexual Misconduct," *Phi Delta Kappa* Fastback 408 (1996).

4. H.J. Cummins, "Student Crushes: Healthy Adoration vs. Victimization," *Minneapolis Star Tribune*, 1 March 1998, Metro edition.

5. Caroline Hendrie, "Abuse by Women Raises Its Own Set of Problems," *Education Week* 2 (December 1998): 1–7.

6. William Fibkins, "Preventing Teacher Sexual Misconduct," *Phi Delta Kappa* Fastback 408 (1996).

7. *Tweedall v. Fritz*, United States District Court of the Southern District of Indiana, Evansville Division 987 F. Supp. 1126; 1997 U.S. Lexis 207066; 77 Fair Empl. Pra. Cas. (BNA) 1777.

8. Charol Shakeshaft, Laurie Mandel, Yolanda Johnson, Janice Sawyer, Mary Ann Hergenrother, and Ellen Barber, "Boys Call Me Cow," *Educational Leadership* (October 1997): 2225.

9. Nan Stein, "Sexual Harassment Meets Zero Tolerance: Life in K–12 Schools," in *2001: A Legal Odyssey* (Cincinnati: Education Law Association, 2001).

10. William Pithers and Alison Gray, "The Other Half of the Story: Children with Sexual Behavior Problems," in *Psychology, Public Policy and the Law* (Washington, D.C.: American Psychiatric Association, 1998).

11. Bernice Sandler, *Educator's Guide to Controlling Sexual Harassment,* (Washington, D.C.: Thompson, 2001).

12. Illinois Coalition Against Sexual Assault, "Facing It: Sexual Abuse Among Children," (Springfield, IL: Department of Children and Family Services, 1996).

13. Ibid.

14. American Psychiatric Association, *Diagnostic and Statistical Manual of Mental Disorders,* 4th ed. (Washington, D.C.: American Psychiatric Association, 2000).

15. William Fibkins, "Preventing Teacher Sexual Misconduct," *Phi Delta Kappa* Fastback 408 (1996).

16. Office of Inspector General, "Retaining Foster Parents" (Washington D.C.: United States Department of Health and Human Services, May 2002).

17. American Psychiatric Association, *Diagnostic and Statistical Manual of Mental Disorders,* 4th ed. (Washington, D.C.: American Psychiatric Association, 2000).

18. Bernice Sandler, *Educator's Guide to Controlling Sexual Harassment* (Washington, D.C.: Thompson, 2001).

19. *Wilson v. Webb,* U.S. Court of Appeals for the Sixth Circuit, 2000 U.S. App. Lexis 23585.

20. Peter McLaren, *Life in Schools* (New York: Pearson, 2003).

21. Office of Civil Rights, *Questions and Answers About Sexual Harassment,* (Washington, D.C.: U. S. Department of Education, 2001).

22. William Eaton, *The Sociology of Mental Disorders* (Westport, CT.: Praeger, 2001).

23. Rolf Muuss, *Theories of Adolescence* (New York: McGraw Hill, 1996).

24. William Eaton, *The Sociology of Mental Disorders* (Westport, CT: Praeger, 2001).

25. Henry Black, *Black's Law Dictionary* (St. Paul, MN: West, 1979).

26. Charol Shakeshaft and Audrey Cohan, "Sexual Abuse of Students by School Personnel," *Phi Delta Kappan* 76 (March 1995): 512, 520.

CHAPTER 3

WORLDLY WISE

■ ■

OVERVIEW

This chapter provides an effective plan to short-circuit *Lolita* situations in the classroom. Implementing an overall plan equips educators and administrators with a foundation for training faculty to respond quickly and effectively to inappropriate student behavior. Additionally, federal guidelines are given for student privacy and written records. The chapter will conclude with law citations that correlate with information presented. Finally, a brief case study is presented to promote discussion and reflection by the reader.

■ ■

OBJECTIVES

After completing this chapter, the reader should be able to:

1. Identify characteristics of seductive student behavior.
2. List seven effective reaction steps.
3. Describe legal implications regarding student privacy.
4. Describe ten steps for successful student-teacher conferences.

5. Describe ten steps for successful parent–teacher conferences.
6. Define target vocabulary.
7. Apply response plan to sample *Lolita* scenario.

■■

IMPORTANT TERMS

advisory personnel: certified school employees who provide counseling services.

Buckley Amendment: now known as the Family Education Rights and Privacy Act of 1974, this legislation secured the rights of parents to view cumulative student files as well as pertinent teacher rating or observation.[1]

documentation: teacher professional notes and papers; written observations.

fiduciary relationships: a person having the duty, created by his undertaking, to act primarily for another's benefit; founded on a trust or confidence.[2]

parent notification: all letters, telephone calls, and conferences with parents.

reasonable action: obligation to meet the "reasonable person" standard as expected in a court of law; a "reasonable woman" standard may be used in cases of alleged sexual harassment.

■■

DO YOU HAVE A PLAN FOR *LOLITA*?

Although most school districts have sexual harassment policies in place, *Lolita* situations may not be considered sexual harassment by your school administration because the harassment is from student to teacher. Schools have plans for fire drills, general assembly, crisis situations, and bad weather, but rarely are teachers given a plan for responding to *Lolita* situations. Faculty, *especially novice teachers*, need formal, specific guidance to support their professional growth. Design-ing a response plan is the collaborative task of school administrators, teachers, and school advisory personnel. Their planning must focus upon several key issues. They include: identification of inappropriate student behavior, documentation formats, a protocol for communicating with parents, counseling interventions, and administrative support of the classroom teacher.

The following response plan is a support framework for teachers and school administrators. When faced with inappropriate student behavior (written or verbal), your reaction must be timely and on target. The following plan will help guide your ethical, professional, and legal response.

1. Document the student behavior.
2. Notify a supervisor of the incident.
3. Confer with the student *in the company* of another teacher or counselor.
4. Never be alone with the student in any setting.
5. If the behavior continues, request to have the student moved to another class or section.
6. If needed, conduct a parent conference in a group setting.
7. Retain originals of all professional notes and documents. Note: Be aware, some civil cases have gone to court *many years* after the alleged sexual misconduct occurred. Keep all of your documentation as long as you teach.

■■■

HOW CAN YOU IDENTIFY INAPPROPRIATE BEHAVIOR?

Inappropriate student behavior may include but is not limited to the following: grooming behaviors, notes or drawings with sexual overtones, double entendre comments, enlisting friends in rumors regarding the teacher, off-color jokes, and personal phone calls to the teacher's home. Wise teachers will react immediately to each situation. A common myth is that only middle level and high school teachers are the targets of unwanted and inappropriate student behavior. That assumption is wrong. Elementary teachers are also vulnerable to *Lolita*.

■■■

WHAT PROOF DO I NEED?

As an educator, you are held to a high standard of conduct. Legal, ethical, and professional mandates converge in your fiduciary relationship with students. This relationship rests on the centuries-old trust that presumes teachers act primarily for the student's benefit. A hallmark of our profession is the expertise to model social norms. The National Education Association code of ethics holds teaching professionals responsible not to "use professional relationships with students for private advantage."[3] Your school and local community expect professional behavior *above reproach*. You are expected to set an example of moral excellence. Your behavior will come under close scrutiny should an allegation of sexual misconduct be leveled at you.

A teacher's word cannot be his or her only defense in an allegation of sexual misconduct. The educator's side of the story must be supported by clear and convincing evidence. Evidence may take many forms. The best evidence comes from several credible eyewitnesses. Unfortunately, the school environment may not offer easy sight lines for colleagues. The next best evidence is a complete *written* account of the inappropriate student behavior and the teacher's consistent, professional attempts to correct it. Professional notes and anecdotal records, however brief, provide proof of ethical intent to help the student in accordance with school district policies. Keeping a record of incidents, originals of notes or drawings, and a summary statement of resolution will demonstrate your competence as professional exemplar.

Documentation is proof of intervention. For example, teachers should record when they identify the seductive behavior, how they communicate that the behavior is inappropriate (in the presence of a qualified educator), when they notify the school administrator, and they should refer the student to advisory personnel. Teachers may include suggestions for a more effective school placement for the student. Each notation builds a platform of proof supporting the classroom teacher. A quick overview of necessary information includes:

1. What happened?
2. Where did it happen?
3. Who was involved?
4. When did it happen?

5. How often has this occurred?
6. How did the conduct affect you (the teacher)?
7. Were there any prior problems with the offending party?
8. To whom did you (the teacher) talk about the incident?
9. Did anyone witness this? If so, who?
10. What was said by you or the student?
11. What other documents might be important (student notes)?[4]

Quickly but carefully recording problematic student behavior will be a first-line defense in case of a false allegation of sexual misconduct.

■■■

ARE YOUR PROFESSIONAL NOTES PRIVATE?

All written records, including anecdotal records, must meet certain criteria outlined in the Buckley Amendment–Family Education Rights and Privacy Act of 1974. This standard requires all records, including "teacher or counselor ratings and observations," to be open for parent inspection and review. For the classroom teacher, this means only *private professional notes* may be kept from the legal guardian. If teachers share professional notes, such as to support a referral to advisory personnel or to inform school administration, the parent or legal representative may inspect them. Simply stated, if the notes are shared for any reason, they become an official record. You must be certain of what you write, include only observable behaviors, and keep the notation neutral in tone.
     Here is an example:

June 10, 2002
During English class, Janey T. commented on the art teacher's "butt." I warned her this was inappropriate behavior and that it was disrespectful to speak of a teacher in that manner. She agreed and promised no further statements. The entire class heard the comment. Joey R. sits to Janey's right-hand side.
                                                                                M. Manos

Keeping notations of such harassing behavior and your immediate response to the student sends the message that this behavior is not funny and it will not be tolerated in school.

■■■■■■■■■■■■■■■■■■■■■■■■■■■■■■■■■■■■■■■

SHOULD YOU HANDLE THIS SITUATION BY YOURSELF?

First, your professional responsibility as a representative of the school district is to refer students who need specialized services to those most qualified to help. The *Lolita* student needs to be referred to advisory personnel. That means a qualified or certified counselor—not simply another teacher. Although many school districts offer a TAP (Teacher Advisory Program), a certified teacher will not meet the legal requirement as a certified counselor. On the other hand, it is acceptable for a certified teacher to serve as a *witness* of a corrective conference.

Second, you must make a school administrator aware of the situation and how you plan to react to the student behavior.[5] You must inform a principal, dean, or assistant principal of the situation. Allow them to view any documentation you have generated. Share the interventions you have in mind. In case of litigation, you will need to show that you were in complete compliance with your official and contractual responsibilities. Beware! Only share information about the student with other faculty members who have a "need to know" or who can add to the successful resolution of the situation. Simply said, there should be no teacher lounge conversations about the student or the behavior. Place no stigma upon a student.

■■■■■■■■■■■■■■■■■■■■■■■■■■■■■■■■■■■■■■■

WHEN SHOULD YOU CONFERENCE WITH THE STUDENT?

Although teachers hone their communication skills daily, you may feel at a loss for words when faced with a *Lolita* situation. Your first response—a slight embarrassment—is the least effective. Students *want* to be considered attractive to a classroom teacher. Teachers are powerful authority figures. Students may need this approval for their self-worth. The hope of being favored by a teacher they already favor may be too much of a temptation for a middle or secondary school student. When student behavior becomes overly friendly, you must respond in a kind but firm manner. Additional interventions may be necessary if the student fails to respond to initial correction.

The option of a change in class setting should be offered to the student early on in the intervention process. Secondary and middle school students are very territorial about friends, and they seek to remain in familiar groups. Using a change in class schedule as an option may be the leverage needed to ensure future cooperation from the student. On the other hand, a change in class setting may be the first choice by a parent or school administrator.

Finally, this is the time for a three-way conference with the student displaying seductive behavior, the teacher, and an advisor/administrator. They must all come to a mutual understanding about past behavior, future actions, and potential disciplinary steps in the event the behavior reoccurs. Usually, this stops the behavior effectively. Legal aspects include the timeliness of the conference, the parties who attended, and the confidentiality of the conference. An effective and timely conference diffuses any civil court action. To prevail in court, plaintiffs must show that school administrators were knowledgeable about the situation but exhibited gross indifference to sexual misconduct or harassment.[6] Furthermore, official reaction must be reasonable, fair, and caring. The three-way conference is clear and convincing proof that no institutional indifference exists.

■ ■

WHAT DO YOU SAY TO THE STUDENT?

The following plan will help you organize your thoughts prior to the three-way conference. Great care should be taken to separate the inappropriate behavior from the greater worth of the individual.[7]

Step One: Select a neutral location *away* from your classroom.

Step Two: Plan no more than 10–15 minutes. The meeting is not intended to encourage a long conversation. You are steering the conference to a definite, clear point—that is, no further behavior with sexual intent will be tolerated from the student.

Step Three: Introduce all parties.

Step Four: Start positively. Compliment the student on his or her academics, dependable work, or class leadership qualities.

Step Five: Describe the inappropriate behavior and show any objects connected to the behavior, such as notes or drawings.

Step Six: Clearly tell the student that his or her behavior is not an acceptable part of the classroom relationship and you trust there will not be a recurrence. Do not say you are flattered or pleased in any way with the special attention. This may be misinterpreted and serve to encourage the behavior rather than extinguish it.

Step Seven: Explain that the only recourse that remains is to conference with a legal guardian or parent *if the behavior is repeated*.

Step Eight: Remind the student that you like having him or her in class and express your hope for a positive school year. Close the conference *without* hugs!

Step Nine: Document results of the conference and have your witness jot down his or her impressions and/or signature.

Step Ten: File notes in your *Lolita* file. Keep the documents from year to year. In fact, allegations of teacher sexual misconduct have been filed 10 to 30 years after the alleged incident.[8]

This conference may be difficult for you, especially if you are overly sensitive about the student's reaction to the warning, but it is an effective way to short-circuit *Lolita*. Ask yourself: Which is more valuable, preventing a student's momentary embarrassment or continuing your professional career?

■■■

WHEN DO YOU TALK TO THE PARENTS?

The final intervention in a *Lolita* situation is direct, formal communication with the parent. Administrators must not defer the disciplinary responsibility. Civil court judges will scrutinize the action taken by the building administrator. This is the perfect time for the principal to add his or her approval to the teacher's response. Should principals abdicate their responsibility for this conference, they will be held accountable in court for their failure to act.[9]

Your building administrators may want to hold this conference prior to changing the daily schedule for the student. Either way, the parent must be notified in writing. This conference is called at the teacher and school's request. This formal conference should include the teacher, school administrator, advisory personnel, and parent. (Note: The student may be included at the most appropriate time. Certainly, this is not at the same time as the teacher or principal is presenting the situation to the parents.) The following plan will help you organize the agenda. Remember, this is not a progress report; it is a disciplinary situation of great importance to the district.

Step One: Select an official location such as *the principal's office*. Take utmost care that there is confidentiality and privacy.

Step Two: Plan no more than 30 minutes. (The topic will catch the parents off guard and they may want a complete briefing about the classroom setting, the teacher's actions, and expectations.)

Step Three: Introduce all parties.

Step Four: Start positively. Compliment the student on his or her academics, dependable work, or class leadership qualities.

Step Five: Describe the inappropriate behavior and show any objects connected to the behavior.

Step Six: Clearly state that no more behavior with sexual overtones will be tolerated from the student. Do not say you are flattered or pleased in any way with the special attention. This may be misinterpreted.

Step Seven: Explain that the only recourse left is to change the student's placement or schedule *if the behavior is repeated*.

Step Eight: At some point in the conference, request the presence of the student. Only after the teacher has left the room should the student be questioned about the seductive behavior. This allows the student to save face and maintain dignity and defuses any tension between the teacher and student. Be sure to allow parental input and goal setting for future student behavior.

Step Nine: Document results of the conference and have all parties jot down their impressions and/or signatures.

Step Ten: File notes in your *Lolita* file. Keep the documents from year to year.

Although the parent conference may be stressful, behavioral goal setting confirms that inappropriate sexual behavior is not accepted in the school setting. This conference demonstrates to faculty, students, community, and the courts that the school environment is a safe place, free from assault behavior.

In summary, civil and criminal courts hold the teaching profession to the immense public trust they have as caretakers of children. All educational personnel are held to high standards. Teachers must show exceptional levels of responsible behavior, kindness, consideration, and personal dignity. They must shun wrongful conduct. This plan provides a framework for dealing with *Lolita* quickly and successfully. When school districts and teachers fail to implement timely measures, they provide an environment favorable for sexual misconduct and tolerate inappropriate student–teacher relationships.[10] As Wittner Bynner once wrote, "The biggest problem in the world would have been solved when it was small." Empowering teachers to be proactive in *Lolita* situations enables school districts to demonstrate high ethical and professional standards and to protect teachers (and themselves) from legal challenge.

■ ■

CASE STUDY

This case study is provided to encourage discussion. The characters and situations are purely fictional.

The student teacher was approached on the first day of school. Several high school students wanted her phone number. She explained that she was placed at the high school for her student teaching. The two boys laughed and walked down the hall. Each day she continued to get whistles and jokes from the two boys. Soon, one of the boys began to bring her a doughnut every day before first period. She was flattered, but unsure how to say the doughnuts were becoming too personal. How could she say that about a doughnut? The student asked his friend to take a Polaroid picture of the student teacher. The boy had the picture enlarged and placed it on the front of his notebook, and hung another copy in his locker. Several students told the novice teacher about the pictures. She did nothing. The student often put his arm around the young teacher and called her his "woman." The final straw for the student teacher was when the young man asked her to accompany him to the high school prom.

After days of worry, she conferred with her cooperating teacher. When the teacher spoke with the high school student, he said the student teacher had called him several times at home and that she returned his affection. The picture in the locker was proof the young teacher favored him. The inscription, "To my favorite student, with all my love" was further proof the student teacher welcomed a romantic relationship with the young man. The student was crestfallen and angry with the young teacher. The abuse the boy and his friend had started now became intolerable. The student teacher was afraid to walk to her car alone. Then the rumor started. The rumor reported she had slept with both young men. It swept though the student population in a single day. As they passed her room, both boys laughed loudly and made derogatory comments. The student teacher asked for a reassignment. She left the high school as soon as possible.

Discussion Questions

- What indicators of inappropriate behavior are present?
- What would have been the most effective plan of action for the student teacher?
- Did the students' behavior meet the description for sexual harassment?
- What disciplinary action should be taken against the two students?
- If you were the university supervisor for this student teacher, what concerns would you have about her fitness to teach?

■■■

NOTES

1. Michael LaMorte, *School Law: Cases and Concepts* (Boston: Allyn and Bacon, 2002).

2. Henry Black, *Black's Law Dictionary* (St. Paul, MN: West, 1979).

3. John Martin Rich, *Professional Ethics in Education* (Springfield, IL: Thomas, 1984).

4. Bernice Sandler, *Educator's Guide to Controlling Sexual Harassment* (Washington, D.C.: Thompson, 2001).

5. Lee Canter, *Assertive Discipline* (Santa Monica, CA.: Canter and Associates, 1992).

6. *Stoneking v. Bradford Area School District*, 856 F. 2nd 594 (3rd. Cir.1988).

7. C.M. Charles, *The Synergistic Classroom* (New York: Longman Press, 2000).

8. *Doe v. Board of Education of Hononegah Community High School District # 207833*, F. Supp. 1366 (U.S. Dist.1993).

9. *City of Canton, Ohio v. Harris*, 489 U.S. 378,388109 S. Ct. 1197,1204, 103 LEd. 2nd 412.

10. *Armstrong v. Lamy et al.* , 938 F. Supp. 1018 (U.S. Dist.1996).

CHAPTER 4

THE AFTERMATH
OF AN ALLEGATION:
THE FIRST FEW HOURS

OVERVIEW

Several forces impact the teacher who is accused of sexual misconduct. First, school district policy may dictate immediate employment changes. For all school districts, the official action taken within a few hours of the allegation will determine the success of future civil suits against the district. Next, serious ethical questions by the community demand informed answers. Finally, professional consequences may extend to the loss of teaching certification. Unbelievably, many teachers trust that their professional association dues will provide them with legal representation at no cost. They learn, to their dismay, that this is not true. In an allegation of sexual misconduct (a criminal charge), no professional association will financially support the educator. Classroom teachers are left confused, ashamed, and unprepared for their role in an intensive investigation of their professional credibility. Finally, a brief case study is presented to promote discussion and reflection by the reader.

■ ■

OBJECTIVES

After completing this chapter, the reader should be able to:

1. Describe the immediate effects on teachers of an allegation of sexual misconduct.
2. Describe the response of a professional education association.
3. Describe the response of a school district.

■ ■

IMPORTANT TERMS

Your knowledge of the following terms is crucial to your ability to understand the events that transpire after an allegation of teacher sexual misconduct.

criminal: dealing with the law of crime; commission of a crime.

defamation: holding a person up to ridicule, scorn, or contempt in a respectable and considerable part of the community; includes both slander and libel; a statement that exposes a person to contempt, hatred, or ridicule.

due process: an orderly proceeding in which a person is served with notice and has an opportunity to be heard and to enforce and protect his or her rights.

evidentiary hearing: a hearing during which evidence is presented for evaluation.

hostile environment: applies when the harassing behavior of anyone in the workplace causes the workplace to become hostile, intimidating, or offensive.[1]

indemnification: contract to which one person secures (insures) another against loss or for some responsibility assumed by another.[2]

legal representation: the right to employ an attorney.

liability: a legal responsibility.

mandated reporter: a person who, in the performance of his or her occupational duties, has reasonable cause to suspect that a child has suffered harm as a result of child abuse or neglect, shall by law immediately report the incident to the child protection agencies.[3]

pariah: an outcast.

polygraph: a mechanism for recording variations in body response, used to validate personal accounts in criminal investigations.

property right: the right to specific property whether it is personal or real property, tangible or intangible. Teachers have a property right to continued employment.

sexual assault: a wide range of victimizations, separate from rape or attempted rape. Includes verbal threats, attacks, or attempted attacks generally involving unwanted sexual contact, that may or may not involve force. This is a felony charge. It may be committed without touching.[4]

sexual battery: a felony charge that includes any unlawful touching of another that is without justification or excuse. The incident may include rape, indecent liberties, child molestation, or sodomy.

witness: a credible person who sees or perceives a thing; a spectator.

■■■

WHAT IS AN ALLEGATION?

One teacher called it a never-ending nightmare. Facing prison, financial ruin, a loss of community standing and retirement benefits, the 60-year-old public school teacher endured 12 months of bearing the shame and disgrace of a public allegation of raping a former student, before the student recanted the claim.[5] Clearly, an allegation of sexual misconduct has immediate and far-ranging effects for the targeted teacher. All school personnel are bound by state law to be mandated reporters of *any* suspected child abuse. This responsibility triggers a sequence of events that will affect all stakeholders in an allegation of teacher sexual misconduct.

The sequence of events, very briefly, will occur according to the following timeline:

1. Student or parent files an allegation of teacher sexual misconduct.
2. Child protection authorities and local police are alerted.
3. Teacher is immediately relieved of all teaching duties and restricted from access to students.
4. Teacher is arrested and held by local police authorities.
5. Teacher is barred from all school activities and properties.
6. Child protection services interview the victim and other students.
7. Child protection services interview the accused teacher and faculty.
8. Simultaneously police interview the victim and other students.
9. Police interview the accused teacher and school administrators.
10. Police provide evidence to state's attorney.
11. A formal charge is made against the teacher.
12. Teacher is officially charged.
13. Teacher enters plea.
14. Teacher's bail is set.
15. Media reports all information contained in grand jury indictment and open court proceedings.
16. School district (depending on collective bargaining agreement and state law) suspends the teacher without pay until further notice.
17. School district begins its in-house investigation.
18. Trial date is set.
19. School year continues.

One teacher remarked that a false allegation of sexual misconduct is the worst thing that could happen to an educator. This is quite an understatement.

Every stakeholder has a specific part to play in the investigation of a teacher sexual misconduct case. The following scenario will vary from state to state and school district to school district. Nevertheless, law and state statutes generally define the roles.

■■

WHAT MUST THE SCHOOL DISTRICT DO?

The school district is required by law to show it took all due care to protect students from further harm.[6] Additionally, the school district is bound by legal precedent and federal sexual harassment laws to demonstrate that it did not "maintain a policy, custom, practice, or common usage that communicated authorization of assault behavior."[7] As a result, the educator can count on five reactions from the school district:

1. The victim's version of events will be taken over the teacher's word.
2. The victim will be not made available to answer questions by the teacher or the teacher's legal counsel.
3. The teacher will be immediately suspended with or without pay, depending on school board policy, collective bargaining agreement, and state law.
4. The teacher will be denied access to students, the classroom, and private materials left in the school.
5. The school district administrators will conduct or arrange to have mental health professionals conduct interviews of *all* students with whom the teacher has daily contact.

The school district has specific guidelines to follow if they wish to show no legal culpability in the actual events or a potential cover-up of the allegations. School policy must be followed to the letter. Many school policies are written to protect the district from any civil suits that most assuredly will follow on the heels of a criminal charge. School policies are crafted to protect the district and the victim, not the educator. The district will stay on the safe side. That means it will deal more stringently with the educator than with the student or concerned community members.

School administrators are well aware of the danger of delaying action until all the facts of the case from the criminal investigation are known. School district administrators may choose to interview students and teachers without advance notice. For example, the National School Board Association suggests that schools should conduct their own investigation, separate from other governmental entities. On the other hand, the district may wish to hire mental health professionals to conduct level-one interviews. School policy is formulated "in the best interest of education of the district." A teacher cannot assume that includes a stalwart defense of all certified employees.[8]

Remember, determination of whether the allegations are credible is based solely on the interview with the student.[9]

Benefits for the school district to conduct level-one interviews include:

1. The ability to judge the allegation in light of student veracity
2. Consideration of the student's prior behavior record
3. Consideration of the context of events (such as a failing grade in the teacher's class)
4. Consideration of the parent's veracity
5. The ability to speak with potential eyewitnesses
6. The ability to videotape or audiotape student responses for future reference
7. The ability to provide the student with a safe, familiar setting for the interview

Disadvantages include:

1. The potential to unknowingly lead a student toward a conclusion
2. The potential to unknowingly provide supporting essential details to a student
3. Conspiracy to protect a faculty member from prosecution
4. The potential to mislead parents as to official school district intent and action
5. The assumption of the faculty member's guilt
6. The generation of evidence potentially damaging to the faculty and district interests

The school district holds a professional and moral responsibility to protect students from harm.[10] Additionally, should the case go to civil court, lawyers, judges and Office of Civil Rights representatives will evaluate the reasonability and accuracy of the initial investigation procedures. Remember, school administrators must always concede credibility to the student.

Professional consultants disagree on the potential liability when school district personnel conduct initial victim interviews. Several experts advise school administrators to bring in outside experts for level-one interviews.[11]

Benefits for the use of outside interviewers include:

1. A clear attempt to keep the interview from being tainted by school politics
2. The ability to select someone professionally trained to interview vulnerable youth
3. The ability to provide a neutral party for both school and community interest
4. A lowered legal culpability for school district administrators (i.e.," no cover up")
5. An interview setting outside the school environment

The school district must display sensitivity and a sense of support to the *victim*. Asking a professional mental health expert or rape counselor to do the initial interview sends the message that school authorities have the student's best interest in mind.

Disadvantages include:

1. A loss of school district control over the situation
2. The appearance that false allegations are deemed credible by community media attention
3. Contact with individuals who may have ulterior motives to find guilt or innocence
4. The potential for information leaks
5. The potential that fearful students in unfamiliar surroundings may make wild statements to bolster a flimsy story,
6. The potential for allegations to become mixed with other community issues (e.g., school funding or accessibility of school administration and school board)

Remember, by federal law, the school district must seek out students who might have additional information in regard to the alleged incident. School authorities must interview all students and adults who have direct contact with the faculty member or the victim.[12]

Whether or not district administrators decide to utilize outside resources for initial investigation, they will eventually complete an in-house investigation to provide evidence for the following decision points:

1. To suspend the faculty member with or without pay
2. To select information appropriate for release to the public
3. To terminate the faculty member's employment contract
4. To compose a final letter of findings to school board members
5. To delay or extend school district findings until all criminal charges are adjudicated
6. To document potential evidence to be used in light of a civil suit against the school district or potential Office of Civil Rights complaint
7. To compose an official response to a written or verbal parent complaint

Evidentiary hearings will be convened at the school district level to meet constitutional mandate. Evidentiary hearings will take place *after* any reassignment, involuntary transfer, or suspension. Although constitutional due process requirements mandate an opportunity for the accused to hear the allegations against them and to answer those allegations, accused teachers may not be able to prove their innocence in a school district hearing. Should the school authorities decide to allow the teacher to continue to work, the circumstances may be so unbearable as to encourage the teacher to resign their professional position. This practice is termed "constructive discharge."[13] The phrase describes working conditions so intolerable as to force a reasonable employee to leave.

During an evidentiary hearing, the teacher or their legal representative is free to call character witnesses, but the teacher will not have an opportunity to question the victim directly. Fears of intimidation and retaliation will most definitely keep victims from appearing at the evidentiary hearing.[14] Such a situation leaves educators in a position where they cannot question their accuser. It is very difficult for an educator to rise above the appearance of guilt when victims cannot be directly and openly questioned.

Finally, no single standard for statute of limitations exists. In cases of delayed memory, alleged sexual assault acts more than 30 years after the fact may be leveled against a teacher.[15] In such cases, accused educators struggle to remember exact details and locate potential eyewitnesses after decades of intervening school years. The accused educator becomes a pariah in the school district and in the surrounding community, with few legal resources. In summary, school districts must attempt to limit their liability for sexual harassment violations, obstruction of a criminal investigation, or for due process violations.

WHAT MUST CHILD PROTECTION SERVICES DO?

State statutes identify school employees as "mandated reporters" in cases of potential child abuse reports. School employees need nothing more than an overheard comment, a rumor, or simple surmise to call child protection agencies.[16] In fact, if they fail to report suspected child abuse, they themselves are liable for criminal charges, loss of state certification, and loss of employment. The child protection authorities *will be involved* from the first whisper of teacher misconduct. State guidelines provide specific requirements for a prompt response by child protection services. Within hours of the initial report, a caseworker will be on the scene working with school authorities and talking with the victims. Children and family services will interview the student and all witnesses—credible or not. They will compile information in regard to the alleged incident and any other concerns students, faculty, and parents may express.

As a result, the educator can count on four reactions from the child protection agencies: specially trained child/youth interviewers will hold extensive sessions with the alleged victim; information about the educator will be sought from fellow faculty and community members; information from the educator's family will be sought; and within days, a report of a "founded or an unfounded" complaint will be issued. If the educator has foster children in his or her home, the children will be immediately removed from the residence until child protection authorities have concluded their investigation. This quick investigation period may not be a boon for the educator. Events may move too quickly for a confused educator to understand and protect their rights. The police will be given all information gained by child protection authorities for grand jury inspection.

■■

WHAT MUST THE POLICE DO?

The police will be involved. Aggravated sexual assault on the part of an educator is a grievous situation for the entire community; it is also a felony crime. The teacher will be arrested, fingerprinted, and held in jail until bail can be set. The teacher will plead either guilty, not guilty, or no contest to the charges. A teacher may request to take a polygraph, with or without the presence of legal counsel. Accused teachers will need to procure their own legal representative. Certified personnel who are members of professional associations will be not be represented by a professional association attorney. In case of a criminal charge, professional associations do not provide legal representation, nor do they offer monetary support until charges are dropped or the teacher is exonerated. However, association members may be guided through an association referral to a competent attorney. Depending on the state attorney's persistence, the investigation may take a fast track to conclusion or it may wait for months. During this time no financial support will be forthcoming for legal fees or court costs from the professional association.

    The sequence of events will not be greatly different whether this is a first or a repeat offense, but the exact sequence will vary from state to state. They include:

1. The first report of a crime by parents, students, or a citizen brings an immediate response from the local police. Most law enforcement agencies will have an officer designated as a Juvenile Sex Offender officer, trained in special interview and investigation techniques.

2. The police follow state regulation on probable cause; that is, they must have good reason to believe a crime has been committed. Police will listen to the student and if there is a preponderance of evidence (51 percent), such as corroborating information that the incident took place, the teacher is arrested.

3. The teacher is taken to a law enforcement center for processing and fingerprinting.

4. The state's attorney will present the investigation findings to a grand jury made up of 24 local citizens. No defense attorney is present at the grand jury deliberation.

5. If the grand jury grants a true bill (clear evidence that the allegation is true), the indictment is returned.
6. A preliminary hearing before a judge in criminal court is set, bail is set, a plea is recorded, and finally, the next hearing date is arranged.
7. A trial date is set and the trial ends with a conviction of guilty or not guilty, unless the student recants the charge of sexual assault or a plea bargain is arranged. Please note the victim will not be expected to give testimony at trial or be expected to pass a polygraph, as this would re-victimize the victim.

Should a teacher be found guilty of a felony charge, there exists the potential of immediate revocation of state teaching credentials and loss of tenure, pension, and other employment benefits. A final facet to the criminal proceedings will be the opening of all records to the general public. Every word of testimony and investigation findings will be accessible from the earliest moment, unless sealed by the judge. In some cases, shortsighted teachers have settled the incident with a plea bargain or perhaps come to a settlement with the school district to resign with benefits. Remember, every word is recorded in open-to-the-public documents and therefore accessible to the media.[17]

■ ■

WHAT WILL THE MEDIA DO?

The media sells papers and TV programs on exciting headlines. Examples include:

"Thirty Years for Teacher in Child-Abuse Case," *The Arizona Republic*, April 16, 2001

"Teacher Accused of Fondling Girl," *The Buffalo News*, January 9, 2001

"Teacher Banned for 'Grooming' Girl for Sex," *The Ottawa Citizen*, April 3, 2001

Need more convincing?

"Public School Probe Expands," *New York Daily News*, May 5, 2001

"Junior High Student Says Gym Teacher Touched Her Repeatedly, Offered Her Money to Disrobe," *St. Louis Post-Dispatch*, March 8, 2001

"State Revokes Three Teachers' Licenses," *Minneapolis Star Tribune*, January 5, 1996

"Ex-Teacher Charged with Child Sex Abuse," *Omaha World-Herald*, May 4, 2001

"Band Director, Student Had Lengthy Affair," *London Times-Mirror*, December 18, 2001

All this, without even mentioning Mary Kay LeTourneau, Julie Anne Feil, or Glenn Harris!

Although headlines do sell papers, they also taint public opinion against teachers. Teachers can be buried in the avalanche of public opinion before they ever appear in court. The television and print media attempt to cover the story within the first few hours. Local media sets a frantic tone during an investigation of teacher sexual misconduct. The community has a strong "knee-jerk" reaction to an allegation; thinking is clouded by the rush of events and public surmise. Inaccurate reporting and explosive comments by community members provide fodder for headlines. For example, a local community newspaper reported an alleged case of teacher sexual misconduct. The teacher's name, home address, and school picture were splashed across the front page. Although school officials declined to comment, the article carried ample quotes from students and parents. The article quoted a parent who wished to "remain unidentified for fear of repercussion from the school." The parent complained, "They [the school board] told the kids to shut up. They totally scared the kids. They don't even want to admit there was a problem. They are too worried about the new middle school [construction project]."[18] Hearsay and surmise, mixed with unrelated issues, fuel public attention.

If media attention inflames community opinion, it also has a potent effect on the victim. Students who lodge a false allegation have scant opportunity to reconsider the consequences of their actions. Worse yet, troubled children swept up in the tide of public outcry may be encouraged to elaborate on their story. For children who exhibit attention-seeking behavior, a false allegation provides an abundance of community attention and empathy.

In summary, aftermath events happen at lightning speed and have far-reaching effects. Teachers must be aware they will be at a financial, professional, legal, and ethical disadvantage in the face of a sexual misconduct charge. Teachers' family members also feel the stigma of such a charge. Community opinion becomes so tainted that living in the same neighborhood may become intolerable for the educator. It is no wonder that many teachers decide to tender a quiet resignation and leave the community rather than seek exoneration in court.

■■■■■■■■■■■■■■■■■■■■■■■■■■■■■■■■■■■■■■

CASE STUDY

The following case study is provided to encourage discussion. The characters and situations are purely fictional.

The band director was surprised to see a female teaching aide enter his morning band practice. She explained that the principal told her to sit in the room until the period ended in 15 minutes. As the bell sounded, students walked out and two local policemen entered the class. They informed the teacher he was being arrested, handcuffed him, and led him out the band room door for questioning at the local police station. The charge was aggravated sexual battery to a minor. In the next five hours, the teacher was informed that a parent had lodged a complaint on behalf of a former elementary school student. The student, who was not a member of the school band, had classes in close proximity of the band hall. The alleged incident had taken place two years before. While at the police station waiting processing, the elementary school principal notified the teacher that he was suspended pending a complete investigation by police authorities, Child Protection Services, and the school district. The teacher was informed that this notice served as verbal confirmation of immediate suspension and that written confirmation would be provided in 24 hours. Under school policy, no district hearing would be scheduled until all criminal investigations were completed.

Discussion Questions

- Why didn't the principal accompany the police to the band hall?
- What was the purpose of school authorities asking a woman teaching aide to sit in the band hall until police authorities could arrest the teacher?

- What factors might inhibit the teachers from contradicting the student's story?
- Might there be an ulterior motive for the allegation?
- Where would the teacher find the approved district time line for due process of this complaint?
- What will happen when the teacher notifies the union representative to request a union-provided attorney to represent him during a police interview?

■■

NOTES

1. Susan Strauss, *Sexual Harassment and Teens* (Minneapolis, MN: Free Spirit, 1992).

2. Henry Black, *Black's Law Dictionary* (St. Paul, MN: West, 1979).

3. Council of School Attorneys, *Child Abuse: Legal Issues for Schools* (Alexandria, VA: National School Boards Association) ERIC Document # ED 435-138.

4. Illinois Coalition Against Sexual Assault, *Facing It: Sexual Abuse Among Children* (Springfield, IL: Department of Child and Family Services, 1996).

5. Caroline Hendrie, "At One California School, A Never-Ending Nightmare," *Education Week* (16 December 1998): 15.

6. *Tweedall v. Fritz*, United States District Court of the Southern District of Indiana, Evansville Division 987 F. Supp. 1126; 1997 U.S. Lexis 207066; 77 Fair Empl. Pra. Cas. (BNA) 1777.

7. *Stoneking v. Bradford Area School District*, United States Court of Appeals for the Third Circuit, 882 F. 2nd 720; 1989 App. Lexis 15711.

8. Council of School Attorneys, *Child Abuse: Legal Issues for Schools* (Alexandria, VA: National School Boards Association) ERIC Document # ED 435-138.

9. Council of School Attorneys, *Child Abuse: Legal Issues for Schools* (Alexandria, VA: National School Boards Association) ERIC Document # ED 435-138.

10. Thomas Sawyer, "Teacher-Student Sexual Harassment," *The Journal of Physical Education, Recreation and Dance* (May 2001): 10.

11. Charol Shakeshaft and Audrey Cohan, "Sexual Abuse of Students by School Personnel," *Phi Delta Kappan* 76 (March 1995): 512–20.

12. Bernice Sandler, *Educator's Guide to Controlling Sexual Harassment* (Washington, D.C.: Thompson, 2001).

13. Henry Black, *Black's Law Dictionary* (St. Paul, MN: West, 1979).

14. Caroline Hendrie, "Principals Face a Delicate Balancing Act in Handling Allegations of Misconduct," *Education Week* (16 December 1998): 14.

15. Caroline Hendrie, "Passing the Trash by School District Frees Sexual Predators to Hunt Again," *Education Week* (9 December 1998): 16, 17.

16. *Tweedall v. Fritz*, United States District Court of the Southern District of Indiana, Evansville Division 987 F. Supp. 1126; 1997 U.S. Lexis 207066; 77 Fair Empl. Pra. Cas. E 1777.

17. Council of School Attorneys, *Child Abuse: Legal Issues for Schools* (Alexandria, VA: National School Boards Association) ERIC Document # ED 435-138.

18. Marina Harris, "Parents: School Veiled Rodney Winkler Incident," *Washington Times Reporter* (Washington, IL), 20 March 2002, 1.

CHAPTER 5

TEACHERS AND THE COURTS: THE FOUR INVESTIGATIONS CONTINUE

■■

OVERVIEW

This chapter will detail the state and local investigations. In addition, ethical issues and certification revocation will also be covered. The focus in this chapter is not to document the investigation of a pedophile masquerading as a teacher, rather it is to describe a teacher *wrongfully accused* of sexual misconduct. The ensuing investigation is a nightmare experience that often ends an outstanding career as an educator. Finally, a brief case study is presented to promote discussion and reflection by the reader.

■■

OBJECTIVES

After completing this chapter, the reader should be able to:

1. Describe the effects of pre-deprivation and post-deprivation due process.
2. Anticipate trial events and testimony.
3. Define criminal charges.

■ ■

IMPORTANT TERMS

Understanding potential criminal charges is the critical element in successfully answering an accusation. Your knowledge of the following terms is crucial to your ability to understand the criminal charge.

accidental contact: contact outside of the teacher's official capacity, such as off-campus with a minor who is not a student.[1]

aggravated sexual assault: a wide range of victimizations, separate from rape or attempted rape; includes verbal threats, attacks or attempted attacks generally involving unwanted sexual contact that may or may not involve force. This is a felony charge. It may be committed without touching.[2]

aggravated sexual battery: a felony charge that includes any unlawful touching of another that is without justification or excuse. The incident may include rape, indecent liberties, child molestation, or sodomy.

child abuse: the physical injury or neglect, mental injury, sexual abuse, sexual molestation, or maltreatment of a child under the age of 18.[3]

coercion: the use of bribes, threats, or intimidation to gain co-operation or compliance.

delayed memory: memory of injury suffered during childhood sexual abuse that is recalled for the first time during adulthood.[4]

discovery: pretrial devices that can be used by one party to obtain facts and information about the case from the other party; opportunity one party has to see the evidence against them.

exploitation: conduct that allows, employs, authorizes, permits, induces, or encourages others to engage in activities that are not in their best interest in order to achieve self-gratification.

felony: a criminal act that would subject the party to imprisonment (note: many state penal or criminal codes have various classes of felonies, with varying sentences for each class).

fondling: touching the genitals, buttocks, or breasts of others for sexual gratification.

frottage: bumping, touching, or rubbing against others for sexual gratification without their knowledge or consent (note: minor children are never considered to have given consent).

improper sexual conduct: any intentional touching or fondling of the victim, either directly or though clothing, for the purpose of sexual gratification.

in loco parentis: schools serve in the place of a parent; charged with parental rights and responsibilities; the official capacity and responsibility of teachers to protect and instruct children.[5]

misconduct: a transgression of some established and definite rule of action; a forbidden act; a dereliction of duty; implies willful or wanton disregard of standards of behavior.

moral turpitude: an act of baseness, vileness, or one that gravely violates moral sentiment or accepted moral standards of community and is culpable in some criminal offenses.

rape: forced sexual intercourse, including psychological coercion as well as physical force.

victim: any person harmed by another.

voyeurism: obtaining sexual gratification from seeing another person disrobed.

■■■■■■■■■■■■■■■■■■■■■■■■■■■■■■■■■■■■■■

HOW WILL THE COMPLAINT BE LODGED?

The complaint that initiates an investigation may take many forms.[6] Reporting avenues include:

1. The student may directly accuse a teacher before school authorities.
2. A student tells another student, who relates the information to school or police authorities.
3. A parent charges the teacher with sexual contact with a minor.
4. A teacher or other mandated reporter overhears a student make a comment.
5. An anonymous letter is sent to school authorities.
6. An anonymous phone call to school administrators identifies a teacher and gives details of the alleged misconduct.
7. A student note describing sexual contact with a teacher is intercepted by other students or teachers.

8. A teacher, student, or community member witnesses inappropriate behavior by the teacher.

9. An untraceable rumor is related to school authorities.

10. A former student recalls a repressed memory of sexual contact with a teacher and reports the incident to school administrators.

Students may report any number of alleged incidents known only to themselves. Student testimony may relate bizarre, infeasible, or completely unsubstantiated incidents. For example, an overview of civil case court documents records student complaints of teacher sexual misconduct that range from sexual molestation (during a class filled with other students), to "a boyfriend-type hug," or being called a "foxy lady."[7] One is left to wonder how some allegations are counted as credible. In fact, all allegations are counted as credible.

■ ■

WHAT WILL THE POLICE INVESTIGATION INVOLVE?

Once an allegation is made, the school district administration will immediately turn the investigation over to the local police. The police authorities will investigate the reported crime. They will interview the victim first. Law enforcement officials are not required to interview the student's parents or other students who could have witnessed the event. Police cannot take into account the victim's prior behavior, inaccuracies in their story, or lack of corroborating evidence. They must be careful not to contaminate victim testimony with leading questions. As a result, a specialist trained in juvenile investigation techniques may be utilized.

Next, based on reasonable cause, police will make an arrest. Reasonable cause to suspect simply means that, based on all the facts and circumstances known to a person, a reasonable person would be led to suspect that the accusation might be valid.[8] It is important to note that teachers might not be interviewed. Once the state's attorney has secured an indictment from the grand jury, a warrant is sworn out for the arrest of the teacher.

School administrators cannot impede a police investigation or arrest without the fear of being charged with obstruction of justice. For example, a principal might ask police not to enter a school classroom to arrest a teacher, fearing such a scene would ignite community opinion. The principal would rather have the teacher report to the privacy of the front office for the arrest. If the teacher flees the building prior to the arrest, the principal has aided the flight of a criminal suspect. As a result, the arrest will happen *when* and *where* the local law enforcement authority deems most efficient.

The police investigation is separate from any other concurrent investigation. Law enforcement authorities follow their own time line for the investigation. Action by local police may hit like a bolt of lightning or may creep along at a slow pace. Finally, in many states, no statutes of limitations are in place for "delayed memory" situations. Teachers may have to answer allegations of sexual misconduct that may have taken place 16–30 years prior to the reporting of the crime.

■■

HOW CAN A TEACHER REFUTE THE CHARGES?

Once notified of the charges, the teacher may request a polygraph test in an attempt to prove innocence. Unfortunately, a lie detector test is not admissible as evidence in court. Polygraphs are not proven to be 100 percent accurate. On the other hand, the victim *will not be asked* to take a polygraph. It is important at this juncture for the teacher to secure legal representation. This is the time for the teacher to share all documentation developed from the "worldly wise" plan outlined in chapter 3. Providing legal counsel with the following materials helps to support the fact that the accused teacher recognized the potential danger of student actions and was proactive. The documentation should include:

> professional notes documenting inappropriate student behavior and comments,
> written notes from the student,
> conference notes,
> the corroborating testimony of other professionals, who witnessed the first three-way conference,
> the teacher's written request that the student be moved to another class.

The use of these materials supports the professional's side of the story and provides knowledgeable witnesses who will be called during the grand jury investigation. Furthermore, the accumulated materials send a clear message that the teacher has fulfilled a professional mandate to seek the student's best interest in all interactions. The teacher's professional notes are admissible in court as supporting evidence *for the educator*.

■■

WHAT EVIDENCE WILL CONVICT A TEACHER OF SEXUAL MISCONDUCT?

Triers of fact will listen closely to the *perceptions* of the victim, examine the findings of the child protection agency, and weigh corroborating evidence. Unfortunately for the accused teacher, the victim may never testify in court. Many states have child testimony guidelines that protect child victims as witnesses. Videotaped testimonies might be presented as evidence, rather than subjecting the child to the stress of open court testimony. Once again, the perception of the victim will be believed over the intent of the teacher. In several cases, a lack of corroborating evidence has failed to exonerate a teacher charged with sexual misconduct. Regardless of an overwhelming number of character witnesses for the teacher, the testimony of the victim is considered more important and as credible. In fact, one court concluded the word of the victim was enough to find the teacher guilty of sexual misconduct.[9] Child abuse laws rightly place the welfare of the victim above the rights of the perpetrator.

■■

WHAT ARE THE CONSEQUENCES IF THE TEACHER IS FOUND GUILTY?

Reactions to a guilty plea or a guilty verdict are serious and far ranging. If the teacher accepts a plea bargain, perhaps a fine and/or probation in exchange for a guilty plea, the teacher's name is posted on a national listing of sex offenders. In some states, the teacher's state teaching license will be automatically revoked, in others only suspended.[10] Once a teacher is found guilty of a felony, school districts will terminate all employment obligations, and state boards of education will suspend the teacher's teaching and rights to any retirement pay. A career is decimated. Teachers may be facing financial ruin as well. A false allegation of sexual misconduct cuts to the heart of a teacher. It is also the kiss of death for those who are unprepared.

■■

WHAT WILL THE INVESTIGATION BY CHILD PROTECTION SERVICES INVOLVE?

Your knowledge of the following terms is crucial to your ability to analyze the Critical Incident Report.

assigned authority: authority implied from holding a particular position, such as a teacher.[11]

child abuse: the physical injury or neglect, mental injury, sexual abuse, sexual molestation, or maltreatment of a child under the age of 18.

intimidation: to frighten another in order to gain that person's compliance; this may involve verbal and/or physical threats.

misconduct: a transgression of some established and definite rule of action; a forbidden act; a dereliction of duty; implies willful or wanton disregard of standards of behavior.

moral turpitude: an act of baseness, vileness, or one that gravely violates moral sentiment or accepted moral standards of community and is culpable in some criminal offenses.

All sexual contact between an adult and a minor is child abuse. No minor can give legal consent for a sexual encounter with an adult. At the report of teacher sexual misconduct, the child protection services will begin a Critical Incident Report of the allegations. The incident will be investigated by a caseworker. Many states have specific time guidelines for each critical stage in the investigation. For example, within 24 hours, a caseworker must interview the student making the allegation. All interviews are kept strictly confidential and may include the caseworker contacting other students, school administrators, faculty members, and community members.

The caseworker seeks evidence or information about the following:

the exact physical behavior,
the context in which the actions happened,

who was present,

where the incident took place.

A Critical Incident Report will end with a final conclusion as to whether the report is founded in truth or not.

One of three results will come from an investigation by a child protection authority.

1. If the report is deemed to be founded, the investigative worker will then refer the report to the local law enforcement agency for investigation and referral for adult prosecution, or for services through probation.
2. If the state Child Protection Service authority determines that an incident does not meet the criteria for child abuse, but does constitute a criminal offense, the case is referred to law enforcement authorities.
3. If the report is deemed unfounded, action against the teacher is ended.

During the investigation, the teacher will be under suspension from his or her teaching or coaching duties.

In summary, child protection authorities work on state-mandated timelines. Reports are investigated with all urgency and confidentiality. The agency is separate from law enforcement. Should Child Protection Services conclude there is no evidence for a founded allegation of sexual misconduct, legal authorities may still choose to continue their actions against the teacher.

■ ■

WHAT WILL THE INVESTIGATION BY THE SCHOOL DISTRICT INVOLVE?

Your knowledge of the following terms is crucial to your ability to analyze the school district action in response to a charge of sexual misconduct.

collective bargaining agreement: the contractual agreement between a union and the school board.

disciplinary action: a response by school board members or their representative that would punish or incur a penalty against an employee.

due process: the constitutional right that protects persons from arbitrary action; teachers must be afforded a fair procedure for hearing and responding to the charges that endanger their continued employment.

evidentiary hearing: a meeting comprising school board members, school administrators, the accused teacher, and legal representation for the purposes of placing all evidence into consideration, those facts which are necessary for the final determination of employment status.[12]

malfeasance: evildoing; any wrongful act or any wrongful conduct that affects performance of official duty; an act for which there is no authority or warrant of law but which a person ought not do at all.

post-deprivation: action taken against the teacher by the school district after the loss of employment or suspension of teaching duties.[13]

pre-deprivation: action taken against the teacher by the school district prior to loss of employment or suspension of teaching duties.

remediation: the opportunity for a teacher to improve his or her teaching effectiveness under direct supervision by a school administrator prior to termination.

termination: the end of all employment opportunities within a district.

Perhaps the first to respond to a charge of teacher sexual misconduct will be a school administrator. Certainly school administrators will be in the spotlight of intense media attention. The action by school leadership taken in the first few hours after a teacher sexual misconduct complaint will impact the morale of every certified employee in the district.[14] On one hand, the environment must be supportive of the victim. On the other hand, a teacher, with a perfect record of service to the district, must be treated fairly and responsibly. The correct path is not easily discerned.

WHEN IS THE TEACHER NOTIFIED OF AN ALLEGATION?

Experts disagree as to whether the school administrator should inform the accused teacher about the allegation immediately. One line of thinking is that contacting the teacher before law enforcement or child protection agencies can become involved allows the teacher time to mount a strong defense.[15] On the other hand, school districts face legal liability if courts perceive inaction on the part of school leaders.[16] Compounding the situation is the fact that the teacher may not be able to secure legal representation during early interviews. Finally, collective bargaining agreements specify exact procedures to be taken when a formal complaint is lodged against a faculty member. Teachers should not waive their right to any mediation or hearing. The early hours after an allegation pose quite a quandary for the school district; therefore most districts will follow their own attorney's plan to limit any future liability for the district. The safest course of action for school districts seems to be immediate teacher suspension with pay, until independent investigations by law enforcement and child protection services are completed.

WHAT ARE THE TEACHER'S OPTIONS?

If school administrators have a Gordian knot to solve, the accused teacher is at far greater disadvantage. All factors converge to shame, discourage, and dishearten the teacher. With little or no pre-deprivation due process, the teacher enters a no-win situation. Initial notice of an allegation might be verbal or written. Perhaps both forms of district notification will happen simultaneously with an arrest. The teacher's absence from school sends the message to the community that the school district believes the allegations are true. The teacher is left with little or no professional support. Accused teachers are barred from school grounds, isolated from fellow faculty members. Union representation is absent until criminal charges are dropped or the teacher is cleared. School records that could supply reasons or motivations for a false allegation cannot be considered as evidence.

The school district might also ask the teacher to suspend post-deprivation due process until it is clear whether there is sufficient evidence for a criminal indictment. Occasionally, students and parents come forward to support the accused during school board meetings. As comforting as it may be to hear someone support the educator, such open-forum confrontations will ensure media coverage. In theory, local media serves as an arena for various opinions. In practice, media coverage will inflame public opinion. Simply said, a career is decimated in the time span of a few days.

The logical next step, for all but the most stalwart educator, is to resign under some sort of mutual termination agreement. The teacher selects a path of least resistance, simply to get out as quickly as possible. Although that step seems the quickest way to end an emotional and professional gauntlet, it is not always in the teacher's best interest, nor is it always possible. Several states have begun to limit a school district's ability to allow a teacher to resign under an allegation of sexual misconduct.[17] For example, California and Michigan restrict school districts from deals cut behind closed doors—deals that might allow teachers accused of sexual misconduct to quietly resign. Some states require school districts to report any case of alleged sexual misconduct to the state board of education.[18]

WHAT IS A DISCIPLINARY HEARING?

For those educators who believe they can outlast the storm and ultimately prove their innocence, the future looms dimly. If the criminal charges are dropped and the child protection agency finds the report unfounded, the school district still may initiate disciplinary action against the teacher. It is important to note that the school district investigation happens independently of law enforcement or child protection agencies. Therefore, in compliance with collective bargaining agreements and set time lines, school districts may still opt to bring disciplinary charges against the accused teacher.

A disciplinary investigation may result in termination, involuntary transfer to a nonteaching placement, a financial penalty, or issuance of a letter of reprimand. A disciplinary hearing may go forward with no corroborating evidence and little more than rumor, assumption, or surmise of teacher misconduct. At no juncture in the disciplinary hearings will the teacher be afforded an opportunity to question the student who lodged the complaint, due to fears the student might be intimidated. School districts may consider past teacher effectiveness and prior complaints from fellow faculty, parents, or students. Also, any prior incident that may show a "pattern of misconduct" on the teacher's work record may be considered, even if it has just come to light. For example, a fellow faculty member may include a complaint against the teacher for an episode that occurred months earlier.[19]

Several concerns will guide school board evaluations of the teacher's fitness to continue teaching and to carry out educators' professional responsibilities in the community. First, can the teacher meet the higher standard of conduct expected for a professional educator? Can the teacher serve as a role model? Next, will the teacher bring an undue level of notoriety to the district? Last, is there a chance the behavior can be remediated or is there a likelihood of recurrence? Be aware that public opinion has a great deal of sway in such matters of notoriety and professional effectiveness.[20] Tenured teachers have a slightly greater chance of holding on to their employment, but probationary teachers or those on short-term contracts are fighting an uphill battle to maintain their faculty position.

In summary, the school district will seek to limit liability in future court action, pacify public reaction, comply with collective bargaining agreements, and meet due process concerns for employment termination. It is important to note that if students were to recant the allegation of sexual misconduct, rarely will they receive any disciplinary action from the school district. Token punishments have been meted out, such as losing recess.[21]

■■

WHAT WILL THE STATE DEPARTMENT OF EDUCATION INVESTIGATION INVOLVE?

Your knowledge of the following terms is crucial to your ability to analyze the state department of education action in response to a charge of sexual misconduct.

> **immoral actions:** actions that do not conform to principles of right conduct.

malfeasance: evildoing; any wrongful act or any wrongful conduct that affects performance of official duty; an act for which there is no authority or warrant of law but which a person ought not to do at all.

professional ethics: an enforced code of uniform rules and behavioral standards by means of which members of the profession are informed of acceptable behavior; concerns public acts by persons in their professional roles.[22]

■■

HOW WILL STATE SCHOOL CODES AFFECT ALLEGATIONS OF TEACHER MISCONDUCT?

Since colonial times, teachers have been held to a high standard of moral conduct within the community. Modern courts have underscored the "special privilege" inherent in a "unique position of trust and authority." A teacher whose behavior "shocks the conscience" is abhorrent to the education community. States have a vested interest to police the ranks of teachers, to remove those who use their teaching authority to harm students or who violate ethics standards adopted by state boards of education. The state board of education issues teacher certification in compliance with the legislated school code, and the state can withdraw that license at any time. License revocation is often the final step in the state education department's investigation of teacher sexual misconduct.

Several states require school districts to report all cases of teacher resignation during investigation of alleged sexual misconduct. Others have professional ethics boards that investigate allegations of misconduct. Acting as an arm of the state board of education, official decisions are final and cannot be appealed. Although presently no comprehensive interstate agreement exists to identify teachers whose licenses were revoked, fingerprinting and background checks are becoming commonplace across the nation. In addition, there are several private agencies that offer school districts access to their database listings of teachers convicted of sexual misconduct. The state will begin an investigation after the school district, law enforcement, and child protection agency action has concluded. Once a state license has been revoked, a teacher may be considered unfit for any teaching position, in any state.

In summary, the emotional, financial, and physical distress endured by teachers wrongfully accused of sexual misconduct is beyond imagination. The stigmatization of being investigated for immoral acts can follow teachers for the rest of their careers and lives. Sadly, students who fabricate wild stories face little or no punishment. Knowing the pace and purpose of each phase of an investigation can help teachers navigate dangerous and deadly professional waters.

■■■

CASE STUDY

This case study is provided for purposes of encouraging discussion. The characters and situations are purely fictional.

A fight between two girls in the hallway summoned a middle school teacher from his classroom. The teacher pulled the girls apart by placing his arms around one student and using the weight of his body to swing the girl away from the confrontation. At the same time, a female teacher stepped between the combatants. After escorting the students to the principal's office, both teachers returned to their respective classrooms. The following week, the male teacher received notification from the school principal that he had been accused of fondling the breasts of one of the girls who had been fighting. The school district imposed a time of administrative suspension with full pay and benefits. Later that day, police arrived at the teacher's house to arrest him pending investigation of three additional complaints. All three girls were friends of the student issuing the initial complaint. The girls reported several complaints such as: "He looked down my blouse, when he stood behind my desk," "He snapped my bra strap," and "He touched my butt as I walked past him to enter his class." This series of allegations began investigation by the child protection agency, law enforcement, and school authorities.

Discussion Questions

- What support will his union attorney provide?
- Will the school investigators consider motivation or prior behavior when evaluating the girls' complaints?

- The teacher can provide several faculty members who will testify to his moral character. Will this be considered in a court of law? To what extent?
- Will the teacher be able to talk to the alleged victims?
- Could other faculty, who may have old grudges, add evidence to the school district investigation?

■ ■

NOTES

1. Council of School Attorneys, *Child Abuse: Legal Issues for Schools* (Alexandria, VA: National School Boards Association) ERIC Document # ED 435-138.

2. Bureau of Justice Statistics, *National Crime Victimization Survey* (Washington, D.C.: U.S. Department of Justice, 2001).

3. Illinois Coalition Against Sexual Assault, "Facing It: Sexual Abuse Among Children" (Springfield, IL: Department of Children and Family Services, 1996).

4. Peter Pashler, *Trying a Case of Sexual Misconduct* (Alexandria, VA: National School Boards Association) ERIC Document # ED 435-138.

5. Henry Black, *Black's Law Dictionary* (St. Paul, MN: West, 1979).

6. Caroline Hendrie, "Principals Face a Delicate Balancing Act in Handling Allegations of Misconduct," *Education Week* (16 December 1998): 14.

7. *Tweedall v. Fritz*, United States District Court of the Southern District of Indiana, Evansville Division 987 F. Supp. 1126; 1997 U.S. Lexis 207066; 77 Fair Empl. Pra. Cas. (BNA) 1777.

8. Henry Black, *Black's Law Dictionary* (St. Paul, MN: West, 1979).

9. Charol Shakeshaft and Audrey Cohan, "Sexual Abuse of Students by School Personnel," *Phi Delta Kappan* 76 (March 1995): 512–20.

10. Phillip O'Connor, "When Teachers Break the Trust," *Kansas City Star*, 24 August 1997, Metropolitan edition, 1.

11. Illinois Coalition Against Sexual Assault, "Facing It: Sexual Abuse Among Children," (Springfield, IL: Department of Children and Family Services, 1996).

12. Henry Black, *Black's Law Dictionary* (St. Paul, MN: West, 1979).

13. Bernice Sandler, *Educator's Guide to Controlling Sexual Harassment* (Washington, D.C.: Thompson, 2001).

14. Charol Shakeshaft and Audrey Cohan, "Sexual Abuse of Students by School Personnel," *Phi Delta Kappan* 76 (March 1995): 512–20.

15. Council of School Attorneys, *Child Abuse: Legal Issues for Schools* (Alexandria, VA: National School Boards Association) ERIC Document # ED 435-138.

16. Bernice Sandler, *Educator's Guide to Controlling Sexual Harassment* (Washington, D.C.: Thompson, 2001).

17. Tim O'Brien, "Teacher's Fight Against Sex Charges Shows Limits of Agency Due Process," *New Jersey Law Journal* (21 May 2001): 1.

18. Phillip O'Connor, "When Teachers Break the Trust," *Kansas City Star*, 24 August 1997, Metropolitan edition, 1.

19. Tim O'Brien, "Teacher's Fight Against Sex Charges Shows Limits of Agency Due Process," *New Jersey Law Journal* (21 May 2001): 1.

20. *Peaster Independent School District v. Glodfelty*, Court of Appeals of Texas, Second District, Fort Worth 63 S.W. 3rd 1 2001: Tex. App. Lexis 3105.

21. "Fourth-Grade Girls Are Fined $5.00 Each for Sex-Abuse Hoax," *St. Louis Past. Dispatch*, 9 May 1998, Five Star Lift edition, 12.

22. John Martin Rich, *Professional Ethics in Education* (Springfield, IL: Thomas, 1984).

CHAPTER 6

THE CIVIL COURT: SCHOOL DISTRICTS AND THEIR TEACHERS

■ ■

OVERVIEW

School boards and their administrators may find themselves facing myriad state and federal civil suits in response to allegations of teacher sexual misconduct. Case law abounds with reports of school boards who made poor decisions and/or attempted to delay or defer decisive action. There is no successful legal defense for school policy that is in noncompliance with the federal constitution or state tort legislation. This chapter lists and describes specific cases from federal and state civil court that involve teacher sexual misconduct.

■ ■

OBJECTIVES

After completing this chapter, the reader should be able to:

1. Define "official capacity" as it relates to teachers and school administrators' performance of their duties.
2. Define "color of law" as it impacts liability for actions taken by teachers and school administrators.

3. Describe several facets of teacher and school district liability in civil court decisions.

■■■

IMPORTANT TERMS

School administrators are presented with a quandary when investigating or responding to allegations of sexual misconduct by fellow administrators or teachers. The student may be in tears, having little or no proof of the allegation; the parents may be confrontational and uncontrollable; the media demands immediate action; school policy may be outdated or absent; legal paths are confusing; the teacher may be in all-out panic, unable to remember essential information. Add to this picture an administrator who has only a few hours to respond in an appropriate manner. From the earliest moments, the actions taken by the school leadership must satisfy the accountability expected in federal and state courts. Your knowledge of the following terms is crucial to your ability to analyze the civil suit documents.

civil suit: a court action brought to gain or recover individual or civil rights or to obtain redress for an alleged noncriminal injustice.

"color of law": action or power clothed with the authority of state.

compensatory damages: also called "actual damages"; money that may be recovered in the courts by a person who has suffered loss, detriment, or injury to person, property, or rights to compensate one's losses.

defamation: untrue statements about another that harms the person's reputation in the community; holding up of a person to ridicule or scorn; that which tends to injure reputation; a statement that exposes a person to contempt or hatred. Teachers may use this to redress loss of employment or reputation from reports regarding unfounded allegations of teacher sexual misconduct.

federal court: a court that hears issues regarding U.S. constitutional or federal statutes violations only.

indemnification: contract to which one person secures (insures) another against loss or for some responsibility assumed by another.

injunctive relief: a remedy issued or granted by a court at the suit of a complainant.

intentional infliction of emotional distress: charged when a person has suffered ongoing harassment; for example, when an institution shows indifference.

liability: a legal responsibility.

malfeasance: commission of an unlawful act.

misfeasance: improper performance of a lawful act.

negligent hiring: charged when the school district fails in its responsibility to hire persons of high moral standing.

negligent supervision: charged when school supervisory personnel fail to provide protection from sexual harassment.

nonfeasance: failure to perform a required duty.

official capacity: duties within the scope of one's employment; actions taken by employees under the auspices of their institutional responsibilities; a way to sue the public entity that the official represents.

punitive damages: monetary awards as punishment for outrageous conduct or to deter future transgressions.

state court: a court that hears issues regarding state constitutional or statute violations only.

substantive evidence: evidence about which, on the whole, reasonable minds would have reached the same conclusion.

suit: a proceeding in a court of law brought by a plaintiff, answered by a respondent.

tort: a private or civil wrong or injury; its three aspects include a legal duty, a breach of duty, and damage as a result.

wrongful discharge: termination for refusal to tolerate sexual harassment.

Civil suits surrounding teacher sexual misconduct episodes tend to center on specific issues. They include: sexual harassment of students, negligent hiring, negligent supervision, constitutional violation for denial of civil rights, the right to safety and liberty, equal protection under the law, free access to the courts, and defamation or slander.

■ ■

WHAT IS SEXUAL HARASSMENT AND CAN IT BE DIRECTED TOWARD TEACHERS?

Although the purpose of this text is to describe wrongful allegations of teacher sexual misconduct, not to describe sexual harassment, it is necessary to utilize certain elements of sexual harassment liability. Legal accountability for school district personnel rests on the district's actions to quickly respond to allegation of teacher sexual misconduct. The two-pronged test for liability in sexual harassment cases, as defined by the Office of Civil Rights, rests on whether there existed a hostile environment or "quid pro quo" harassment. Courts and the Office of Civil Rights have described a hostile environment as "an environment that occurs when unwelcome conduct of a sexual nature is so severe, persistent or pervasive that it affects one's ability to participate in or benefit from a person's work, education program or activity, or create an intimidating, threatening or abusive educational environment."[1]

Quid pro quo usually describes an improper use of power in a "something given or something withheld in exchange" relationship. Quid pro quo is defined by the Equal Employment Opportunity Commission as sexual harassment that involves submission for sexual demands that are made either explicitly or implicitly as a term or condition of employment or advancement, or submission to sexual demands made a basis for decisions affecting a person's employment or academic standing.[2]

It seems improbable that quid pro quo sexual harassment would impact wrongful allegations of teacher sexual misconduct, unless extortion was involved. On the other hand, a hostile environment does exist when a teacher is repeatedly subjected to degrading comments or actions by students. Teachers who are targeted by students for such comments must have the support of school leadership. Further, the responsibility for disciplinary action toward such students must not be placed on the teacher's shoulders. Students who sexually harass teachers must be referred to school administrators for prompt, effective disciplinary action. Courts will question whether the school administration, once made aware of a sexual harassment situation, allowed an abusive working environment for the teacher to continue. Such inaction would evidence deliberate indifference by the school district. School leadership must not construct an atmosphere hostile to teacher complaints of sexual harassment by students.

■■

WHAT LAWS GUIDE SCHOOL DISTRICT SEXUAL HARASSMENT POLICY?

School districts must meet several mandates to control sexual harassment situations, whether it occurs student to student or student to teacher. Presently, school districts are curbed by federal court rulings under the U.S. Constitution; federal, state, or local laws and rulings; Office of Civil Rights guidance policy; Equal Employment Opportunity Office guidance policy; and collective bargaining agreements.

Legislative and constitutional mandates redressing sexual harassment include the following:

Title VII of the Civil Rights Act of 1964: This legislation, enforced by the Equal Employment Opportunity Commission, permits victims of employment discrimination based upon race, color, national origin, religion, or sex to collect compensatory damages for sexual harassment (a form of sexual discrimination). Several policy guidance papers are available for school administrators from the Equal Employment Opportunity Commission. Remedies may include injunctive relief and compensatory and punitive damages, within limitations.

Civil Rights Act of 1991: Legislators amended Title VII to permit victims to add punitive damages for mental distress due to sexual harassment. Victims may request back pay, front pay, and actual out-of-pocket expenses. Enforced by the Equal Employment Opportunity Commission, cases may be resolved through intergovernmental agreement and cooperation with the school district, or action through the U.S. Department of Justice, seeking injunctive relief. Remedies may include monetary damages such as wages and job-connected losses, reinstatement and/or promotion, and compensation for attorney's fees.

Title IX of the Education Amendments of 1972: This legislation covers all institutions receiving federal aid. This federal statute is enforced by the Office of Civil Rights and protects victims of sex discrimination. The revised 2001 Office of Civil Rights policy guidance on sexual harassment situations provides standards of determining an institution's liability. The Office of Civil Rights provides guidelines for grievance procedure, filing a complaint, investigation procedure, program definitions and limitations, time limits for filing, confidentiality issues, and compliance reviews of the school district. Remedies include monetary damages for suffering and emotional distress, future medical or therapeutic costs, attorney's fees, wages and job-related losses; reinstatement or promotion; tuition refunds; and injunctive relief requiring schools to change policy or training policy. It is important to note that even if plaintiffs lose in a court decision, they may file a complaint with the Office of Civil Rights.

Title 42 under the United States Code, Section 1983: This law protects anyone acting "under color of law" from depriving individuals of any right secured by the U.S. Constitution. Section 1983 allows plaintiffs to be heard in a federal court. Allegations of harassment or personal injury by state employees in the performance of their jobs hold both individuals and institutions liable. Remedies include compensatory and punitive damages along with injunctive relief.

U.S. Constitution, Fourteenth Amendment—Equal Protection Clause: Cases brought under this federal protection includes public institutional liability for intentional sexual harassment. Also included here is the issue of equal access to remedies in courts of law. School employees who do not provide accurate information regarding appeal of school policy decisions restrict equal access.[3] Remedies include compensatory and punitive damages along with injunctive relief.

U.S. Constitution, Fourteenth Amendment—Due Process Clause: Due process of law implies the right of a person to be heard and to have the right to refute every material fact that bears on the question of life, liberty, or property (employment). Teachers who lose employment as a result of wrongful allegations of sexual misconduct may seek relief from due process violations. Remedies include compensatory and punitive damages along with injunctive relief.

U.S. Constitution, Fourteenth Amendment—Protected Liberty:
U.S. citizens have a right to a protected liberty of bodily integrity. Used in sexual abuse allegations, this describes the right to be protected from physical harm. In loco parentis includes the responsibility of the schools, as temporary parents, to protect students from physical harm. Remedies include compensatory and punitive damages along with injunctive relief.

Section 504 of the Rehabilitation Act of 1973—P.L. 93-112:
This mandate requires school administrators to carefully consider disciplinary action against any disabled student who might be involved in teacher sexual harassment.

National Labor Relations Act: This law protects teachers who are disciplined or terminated because they attempted to hold meetings around student allegations of teacher sexual misconduct. The National Labor Relations Act protects employees who undertake to improve sexual harassment policies within the school district.

State laws: These laws may also include antidiscrimination statutes that apply to students, school district administrators, and teachers. Fair employment practice guidelines vary considerably from state to state. Equal Employment Opportunity Commission policies are often found in state Fair Employment Practice guidelines. Remedies and time lines differ from state to state.

State education codes: These vary from state to state. Some states include a statement of professional ethics that allow termination or suspension of teacher certificates for moral turpitude or immortality, based on community standards.

Civil cases in state court: Students or teachers may file a suit in civil court (one party seeking damage against another). Common examples of civil suits include the following elements: defamation, wrongful discharge, negligent supervision, and negligent hiring.

Finally, acting as representatives of a governmental entity (a school board), school administrators may incur liability for malfeasance, misfeasance, or nonfeasance within the scope of their professional duties. The community holds schools and teachers to a high standard of conduct in their individual and official capacity. Actions by school personnel that would "shock the conscience of reasonable persons," may result in huge punitive damages awarded by juries.[4] In summary, school administrators are expected to exhibit clear thinking, fair practices, effective communication skills, and an in-depth knowledge of legal liabilities of alleged sexual misconduct, along with an understanding of the repercussions for the faculty and community—not a simple task, by any means.

■■

WHAT CIVIL CASES OFFER PRECEDENTS FOR JUDICIAL ACTION?

Case law reveals the continuum of judicial decisions regarding school administration and teacher sexual misconduct. Legal precedents should drive the formulation or revision of school district policy. Below are some key questions and answers for teachers, followed by the legal cases that set the precedent.

Have teachers who are falsely accused taken the school district to court?

Yes, teachers who are not offered procedural due process in the face of wrongful allegations of sexual misconduct have been given the right of redress by certain state courts. *Flynn v. Riechardt*, Md. Ct. Spec. App., No. 757 (April 3, 2000)

Can a school district be held liable for sexual abuse perpetrated by a teacher?

Yes, school officials who respond with "deliberate indifference" to a known sexual abuse situation are held accountable for the sexual harassment. *Gebser v. Lago Vista Independent School District*, Supreme Court of the United States, 1998 524 U.S. 274

Can a student rumor be the impetus for a report of sexual misconduct against a teacher?

Yes, even accidental physical contact may be enough for school personnel to file a report with child protection services or central office administration. *Wilson v. Webb*, U.S. Court of Appeals for the Sixth Circuit, 2000 U.S. App. Lexis 23585

Will students who falsely accuse a teacher of sexual misconduct be held accountable for falsely reporting a crime?

Probably not, depending on the state statute. Usually students do not report the crime. A school district–mandated reporter does. Therefore, students who lie during investigation or give false information to police are not considered juvenile offenders for having falsely reported a crime. *In* re *Heather B.,* Md. No. 90, Sept. Term 2001, June 7, 2002

How does a "pattern of behavior" relate to terminating a teacher for misconduct?

School districts may be required to show a history of *inappropriate* behavior by the teacher. Examples may include suggestive comments made to fellow faculty members, offensive comments made to minors, or any suspicious physical contact with any child. *Doe v. Gooden,* United States Court of Appeals for the Eight Circuit, 214 F. 3rd 952; 2000 U.S. App. Lexis 12040

Can teachers who use vulgar language be prosecuted for misconduct?

Yes, vulgarity, flirting, sexual comments, and or jokes, especially those meant to demean in a sexual manner, are considered sexual harassment of a student. *Doe v. Gooden,* United State Court of Appeals for the Eighth Circuit 214 F. 3rd 952; 2000 U.S. App. Lexis 12040

Must school district administrators tell parents about further appeal processes regarding allegations of sexual misconduct?

Yes, the Office of Civil Rights is available to help students who complain of sexual harassment regardless of whether criminal charges are filed. School administrators who fail to offer this information to parents are lax in their legal responsibility to provide an environment free of retaliation, hostility, or intimidation for those who report sexual harassment. *Doe v. Berkley County School District,* United States District Court for the District of South Carolina, Charleston Division 989 F. Supp. 768: 1997 U.S. Dist. Lexis 21100

Are school administrators held responsible for teacher action in alleged sexual misconduct cases?

Perhaps, if the school administrators knew of the situation and failed to act. This occurs when school districts fail to follow appropriate administrative policy, fail to protect students from any potential harm, fail to investigate, and/or exhibit indifference to the complaint. *Stoneking v. Bradford Area School District,* United States Court of Appeals for the Third Circuit, 882 F. 2nd 720; 1989 App. Lexis 15711

Will all student complaints regarding improper teacher conduct be placed in the teacher's personnel file?

Yes, a school administrator who receives a formal complaint from a student or parent must place a record of that complaint in the teacher's personnel file. To place it in any other location would be considered active *concealment* of misconduct. Active concealment of prior misconduct would most certainly facilitate an environment favorable to sexual harassment. In fact, inaction on the part of the principal and superintendent may communicate tacit approval of sexual harassment in a court of law. *Stoneking v. Bradford Area School District,* United States Court of Appeals for the Third Circuit, 882 F. 2nd 720; 1989 App. Lexis 15711

How long a time period will students have to report allegations of sexual misconduct?

The response time varies from state to state. In some states, there is no statute of limitations for sexual misconduct allegations against tenured teachers. Many states have special tolling provisions for victims of sexual abuse that considerably extend the period for criminal charges to be filed. In others, the statute of limitations begins when the student becomes an adult. A repressed or "delayed" memory of sexual abuse may also postpone criminal action until *the victim is aware* of the injuries incurred. Courts have not agreed on the exact time period for criminal or civil action against the accused teacher. In addition, a state department of education action against a certified teacher may come at any time a teaching certificate is in effect. *Doe v. Board of Education of Hononegah Community High School District # 207,* United States District Court for the Northern District of Illinois, Western Division 833 F. Supp. 1366: 1993 U.S. Dist. Lexis 13881

Will a school district require a public apology from a student who admits he or she falsely filed a charge of teacher sexual misconduct?

Probably not. The district itself may issue a statement of exoneration, but to require the student to give a public or private statement would construct an atmosphere of intimidation and have a chilling effect on any future allegations of teacher-to-student sexual harassment or sexual abuse. *Stoneking v. Bradford Area School District,* United States Court of Appeals for the Third Circuit, 882 F. 2nd 720; 1989 App. Lexis 15711

As state employees, are teachers and school administrators who serve "in loco parentis" held liable for actions taken in their "official" duties?

Yes, in cases of teacher sexual misconduct, the teacher is outside the "color of law." Neither the local school board nor the state will indemnify action taken to deprive a student of rights confirmed by federal constitution or statutory law. This includes the right to be "safe in personal and bodily integrity." *Canty v. Old Rochester Regional School District,* United States District Court for the District of Massachusetts, 54. F. Supp. 2nd 66; 1999 U.S. Dist. Lexis 9751

When will civil courts use the "shocks the conscience" standard to determine punitive damages to victims?

If a teacher's actions are so grossly excessive as to be shocking to the conscience of a reasonable person, those actions violate substantive due process rights, without regard to state remedies. Punitive damages against the teacher will be based on this question. Did the teacher's actions amount to "brutal and inhumane abuse of official power, literally shocking the conscience" of reasonable persons? Sexual misconduct perpetrated by educators always meets the "shocks the conscience" standard. *Garcia by Garcia v. Miera,* United States Court of Appeals, 1987. 817 F. 2nd 650. *Doe v. Taylor Independent School Dist.,* 15 F. 3rd 443. 445 (5th Cir. 1994)

Can the working conditions for a teacher accused of sexual misconduct become so difficult that continued employment is impossible? Can a change in assignment come even if the school district never officially concludes allegations of teacher sexual misconduct are correct?

Yes, if the employer has made the working condition *so* intolerable as to force a reasonable employee to leave, it is termed a "constructive discharge." Such changes in employment may be part of a settlement agreement. Teachers need to be sure they have followed the collective bargaining agreement time lines and criteria for forced or voluntary transfer. *Tweedall v. Fritz,* United

States District Court of the Southern District of Indiana, Evansville Division 987 F. Supp. 1126; 1997 U.S. Lexis 207066; 77 Fair Empl. Pra. Cas. (BNA) 1777

Could false allegations of sexual misconduct ever be considered sexual harassment by school authorities toward the teacher?

No. Claims of sexual harassment must meet Title IX guidelines. *Tweedall v. Fritz,* United States District Court of the Southern District of Indiana, Evansville Division 987 F. Supp. 1126; 1997 U.S. Lexis 207066; 77 Fair Empl. Pra. Cas. (BNA) 1777

Will a school district be held liable for failure to supervise or carry out written policies prohibiting teacher-student sexual contact?

Yes. A local government entity can be found liable for failing to supervise its employees to prevent or stop sexual misconduct. This liability may also be incurred due to failure to train employees to report and prevent sexual abuse. This case may also have impact on negligent hiring practices. *Armstrong v. Lamy,* United States District Court for the District of Massachusetts 938 F. Supp. 1018; 1996 U.S. District. Lexis 13633

If a teacher resigns due to an allegation of sexual misconduct, are school districts required to share that information with any potential employers of that teacher?

Perhaps. Many states have enacted legislation restricting schools from entering into settlement agreements with teachers accused of sexual misconduct and requiring school districts to disclose the reasons for any subsequent resignations. Due to the verbal nature of job references, negative references might be considered simply hearsay. *Kaylor v. Atwell,* 553 S.E. 2nd 868 (Ga. Ct. App. 2001)

Could a teacher be fired or not be renewed for "diminished effectiveness" to teach or for exhibiting a "disturbing influence on students" as a result of rumors or publicity stemming from sexual misconduct allegations?

Perhaps. Nonrenewal of teaching contracts may be upheld by courts depending on the wording of the school district's policy and compliance with due process requirements and substantive evidence review. A district must have clearly determined criteria for not renewing a teacher's contact. Nonetheless, first-year teachers and nontenured teachers serve at the discretion of the board. *Peaster Independent School District v. Glodfelty*, Court of Appeals of Texas, Second District, Fort Worth 63 S.W. 3rd 1 2001: Tex. App. Lexis 3105

Could a single allegation, even after many years of high-quality, professional teaching, end employment for school personnel?

Yes.

In summary, teachers and schools have much to lose in civil court cases that may drag on for years. An overview of applicable case law reveals the unfortunate fact that school districts and their faculties need advance training in potential legal liabilities and responsibilities. School administrators who fail to train employees regarding actions that constitute sexual harassment do a tremendous disservice to their employees, constituents, school boards, and, most important, their students.

■■

NOTES

1. Office of Civil Rights, "Questions and Answers about Sexual Harassment" (Washington, D.C.: U.S. Department of Education, 2001).
2. Bernice Sandler, *Educator's Guide to Controlling Sexual Harassment* (Washington, D.C.: Thompson, 2001).
3. *Garcia by Garcia v. Miera*, United States Court of Appeals, 1987. 817 F. 2nd 650.
4. *Doe v. Berkley County School District*, United States District Court for the District of South Carolina, Charleston Division 989 F. Supp. 768: 1997 U.S. Dist. Lexis 21100.

CHAPTER 7

MEETING THE CHALLENGE: EXPERIENCE, PERCEPTIONS, IMPRESSIONS

■■■■■■■■■■■■■■■■■■■■■■■■■■■■■■■■■■■■■

OVERVIEW

This chapter will bring together the legal, ethical, and professional standards via first-person accounts of "Educating Lolita" in the class-room. Interviews, case studies, and news accounts of teacher sexual misconduct give readers an opportunity to discuss the issues and li-abilities of adolescent sexual behavior toward teaching professionals. This chapter provides suggestions for in-service presentations, discus-sion, and school policy evaluation. In addition, the chapter includes several discussion questions to facilitate large- and small-group inter-action.

■■■■■■■■■■■■■■■■■■■■■■■■■■■■■■■■■■■■■

OBJECTIVES

After completing this chapter, the reader should be able to:

1. Discuss each scenario in a group setting and identify prob-lematic student behavior.

2. Connect each scenario to a step in the "worldly wise" response plan outlined in chapter 3.

3. Identify student actions that would meet the criteria for sexual harassment.

4. Share an effective teacher response that would meet court scrutiny.

- -

CASE STUDIES

The following case studies come directly from civil cases of alleged teacher sexual misconduct. In each case, the reader will find problematic behavior.

- It Happened to Me: Student makes allegation out of anger for prior discipline action

A high school student teacher writes:

I have a student who is an ongoing problem. He is in the class right after lunch. Every time my cooperating teacher is gone, there is a continuous problem with him. He swears, talks, is disrespectful and refuses to go to work. I sent him to the dean's office. He returned and threw the referral paper at me. I am a student teacher. I can't afford to fail my student placement so I took extra effort to get to know him and show him I am a good teacher. The next week, I overheard him saying that I was being nice to him because I wanted to have sex with him. The rest of the boys laughed, but I know it is a dangerous situation. I can't talk to the student because he is so volatile. His temper fits are something to see. He is derogatory to women and I know he called me a "bitch" and a "whore" in a note to another student. Now he has added this to his boasting, that I am flirting with him. I'm not sure what to do. I know the principal will not take a student teacher's word about what I overheard. How can I go to the parents with no evidence? The faculty says his parents haven't been to a parent conference for years. I don't want to have my university supervisor find out about this. I am having trouble with discipline in all my classes.

- Student makes allegation in attempt to extort money

A teacher with 20 years of teaching experience at a junior high school writes:

It was right around the time the [first] Michael Jackson child molestation case came out in the newspapers, one of my students made an allegation that I had exposed myself to them. The student and I get along well, but I don't know the parents at all. The student and the parent allege the incident happened in my science supply cupboard at school, during my lunch time. I received an immediate verbal suspension with pay, until the whole thing could be "worked out." I was arrested at my home and spent the night in jail. It was not until I received written notification of the charges that I noticed the date of the alleged incident. I was at a teacher professional workshop about state science standards the entire day. Why didn't the school administration check the date before my suspension? When police informed the parents the crime couldn't have happened because I was not even at school, the student tried to say I had returned to school during lunch time to commit the crime. I was in the state capital, an hour away. Why did the kid lie about me? I can only guess they hoped for a money settlement. Our community is low income—we have a lot of kids on free lunch. I guess poverty changes perspectives. The student left the school the next week. I never got an apology from anyone. I still hear negative comments every once in a while. I don't think I'll ever be free of the rumors. I only have five more years [untill I] retire. I hope I can make it.

- Student makes allegation in attempt to have teacher fired

An elementary school teacher writes:

I have a student in class who is a straight "A" student. I think she believes she will always be a straight "A" student. She becomes very angry when she misses a question and argues with me or other students who mark her answers wrong. She has encouraged her parents to complain every time a spelling word is marked wrong on a trial test, because I couldn't read her writing. This girl did not receive an "A" on her 6-week social studies project. She was furious. I don't know how a 5th grader can be so immature. The next day she told her mother I had rubbed her back, moved her shirt up and down, and touched her skin. The parents went to the superintendent's office to file a complaint against me. I was suspended immediately. How can I prove I wasn't inappropriate in my actions toward this student? The word of the student is being taken as fact. The incident happened in a class filled with other students. The police, child protection case worker, and the school district have interviewed every student in my class about the incident. This is a nightmare. What do I do now? How can I go back into that job and teach that class? All the effort I have put into that great bunch of kids is lost forever.

- A student makes an allegation out of misplaced affection

A ten-year teaching and coaching veteran writes:

I have one student who hangs around after practice. This student is eager to help me put away equipment and clean up. I know some students do not want to go home, but this student seemed to have a crush on me. I get Valentine's Day cards from her, and when her family goes on vacation, she brings me a souvenir. Sometimes she calls me her dad. After the game, I took this student home from the game. I stopped to get gas and I bought her a candy bar and a soda pop. The next day, the student told her friends that we kissed in the car. Worse yet, she says this has been going on for quite a while. The parents are uncontrollable. I don't think the student knows what she is saying. The student has shown her friends typed notes she says are from me. The notes are fakes, but I haven't seen them to be able to answer the allegation. I was suspended without pay. If this is the way the school district repays my loyalty and hard work, I just won't teach anymore. I can make more money in construction. I guess my coaching days are ended.

- Student behavior is ignored by school administration

A local police officer who teaches in the school as part of a law enforcement program writes:

I teach each week in several sixth-grade classrooms. In one class, I have a sixth-grade student who has been retained twice—that makes her about 13 years old. She is more mature physically than most sixth-grade students. We do a lot of group work during each class. I like to sit in a student desk while I confer with each group. Each time I work with her group, she stands behind me and leans on my back, with her arms on my shoulders. This is very inappropriate because she is touching my back with her chest. I am used to kids who like to hug, but this is way beyond a hug. I have asked her to stop. I also brought this to the attention of the teacher and the principal. Both feel it is completely innocent and that I am overreacting. I documented the incidents in my lesson plan book. I never sit when I am around her group. I have two careers to think about—teaching and law enforcement.

- A young teacher is threatened by a hostile environment

A first-year teacher writes:

I can't believe the attention I got from the first day in the middle school. The middle school boys were laughing with other teachers, saying they wanted to be transferred into my class because they think I am attractive. Several boys walked in and out of my room during passing period saying, "Oops, sorry, wrong class." In the faculty lounge, the men teachers continue the attitude of the middle school boys and tease me about my looks. I worked hard for my college degree and I want to be treated with more respect. Several days ago, I found "I love you" notes, complete with lewd drawings, left on my desk. Yesterday, someone placed a used condom inside a teacher text I use. I was so embarrassed, I almost had to leave. I don't feel comfortable going to the principal about the situation. I think I know which groups of students are responsible, but I am not sure. Not sure enough to call parents. I'm afraid to go to the male teachers and I am not confident I would have the support of the administration. I starting to be afraid to stay after school, some of these 8th grade boys are quite mature. I have no problems with discipline in class, and my lessons are going very well—but no one prepared me for this situation. I feel lost and confused.

Discussion Questions

In the above scenarios, teachers find themselves in the middle of no-win situations. Using each as a discussion starter, teachers should identify the liabilities and the potential for student allegations of sexual misconduct and answer the following questions:

- What facts (not hearsay) are present?
- As a school administrator, what action is best for the school district?
- What rights will the teacher have in each case?

- If there were a compromise for each situation, what would it entail?
- What experts must be brought into the situation as resources?
- What would the role of the media be in each case?
- Is there a way for the teachers to regain their professional reputations?

■■

NEWS HEADLINES

The media has a role to play in each case of teacher sexual misconduct. The media can provide an open forum for other students who may have been assaulted by the teacher in the past. Students who were assaulted by a pedophile and did not report the crime for fear of reprisal may see things more clearly years later and seek redress. Media coverage also helps to keep the public informed. The dark side to open-forum opportunities is the tendency to rush the public to judgment. Teachers accused of sexual misconduct are often treated in the same manner as a convicted pedophile. The following newspaper accounts are given as a sample of what teachers can expect to see in future cases. The news accounts are greatly abbreviated.

Case One: Elementary Level

Headline: *New York Newsday*, June 23, 1999, page A30, by Willoughby Mariano, "Girl, 10, Testifies about Fondling/Alleges Abuse by 3rd-grade Teacher"

> Questions over exact times and the order of events took center stage yesterday during a sexual abuse trial as a 10-year-old Ronkonkoma girl testified that her former third-grade teacher fondled her in a classroom . . . while other students were at lunch. Questions about the consistency of her testimony arose when the student claimed another fourth-grade teacher at the school interrupted the alleged incident. Under questioning, the student testified . . . she hid in a room while the two teachers talked. Prior statements made by the student in deposition did not agree with her court testimony. In court, the student confused details and changed her story. (The fourth-grade teacher reported he never

entered the classroom during the lunch period.) Surrounded by his family, church members and fellow teachers, [the teacher] heard his former student recount how he allegedly fondled her two years ago.

If convicted, the accused teacher faces a maximum of three to seven years in prison, not to mention the loss of his employment and state teaching certification and being stigmatized the rest of his life.

Case Two: Middle School Level

Headline: *St. Louis Post-Dispatch*, March 8, 2001, page B4, by Robert Goodrich, "Junior High Student Says Gym Teacher Touched Her Repeatedly, Offered Her Money to Disrobe; but Says She Made Up Stories and Was Angry with the Man"

> Junior-high gym teacher . . . is on trial in circuit court in Belleville on a charge of sexual abuse. If convicted, he could be sentenced to up to one year in jail. He could also lose his license to teach. The girl testified that [the teacher] made sexual approaches last February in the gym office. She acknowledged that teachers and students regularly came in and out of the unlocked gym office where she said the teacher's actions took place and that another teacher was just outside the door. The attorney emphasized discrepancies in dates and exact locations between the girl's testimony Wednesday and her statement last March. The attorney identified two former classmates who would testify that the girl had offered each $50 if they would support the allegations against [the teacher]. [The teacher] has been suspended without pay. The girl's mother has filed a civil suit against [the teacher].

Case Three: High School Level

Headline: *London Times-Mirror*, December 18, 2001, by Jon Echtenkamp, "Band Director Student Has Lengthy Affair, Records Indicate"
    Note: A search warrant affidavit and arrest warrant were used to provide the following information to community readers.

> The affidavit contains allegations of [the teacher's] behavior based on interviews investigators had with one of the alleged victims.

The affidavit contains no information about the other alleged victim. Their names are confidential because of state law protecting
the identities of crime victims under the age of 18. The encoun-
ters began in March 2001 and included sexual activity between
the teacher and the 16-year-old girl, in his office, the band room,
the storage room and the school auditorium, during school hours
and even on one Saturday afternoon.... The affidavit describes
an escalating relationship that began when the girl was in eighth
grade and developed into "flirtatious behavior" that ultimately led
to alleged sexual contact with the teacher on several occasions.
The teacher was arrested on two felony counts of taking indecent liberties with children stemming from allegations involving
two 17-year-old students. The charges carry possible prison sentences of one to five years. The teacher [entered an innocent plea,]
posted $10,000.00 bond and faces a Jan. 3, 2002, hearing. Records
indicate [the teacher] is married, has a 3-year-old child and has
no prior criminal record. School officials said they learned of the
allegations against [the teacher] after school Oct. 18, 2001, and
immediately notified police and child care social workers. The
school placed [the teacher] on administrative leave. He resigned
Nov. 13, 2001.

Keep in mind that the information in the article represents just one
side of the story. School officials met every legal mandate in this case.
A troubling element of this case is that two victims brought the charge,
but only one provided information regarding alleged sexual misconduct.

Case Four: Special Education

Headline: *Washington Times-Reporter*, March 20, 2002, page 1, by
Marina Harris, "Parents, School Veiled (Teacher's Name) Incident"

A district special education teacher was charged March 5, 2002,
with aggravated criminal sexual abuse of a 14-year-old middle
school student, a court file said. Everyone at the school was told
not to talk about it, some parents said. This is the only reported
case, but if the public were made more aware, there may be other
kids (with similar stories), said a relative of the student. The
student's relative also said she trusts the student's story because
it cost him hours of interviews with police and officials. "I don't
think any student would put themselves in a position of being

exposed to the embarrassment (if he fabricated the facts)," she said. According to court records, [the teacher] doesn't have any history with the police. [The teacher] pled not guilty and declined to comment.... He was released a day after his arrest and posted $25,000.00 bond, with the condition to have no contact with minors and the victim.

This story, spiced with comments from the public, leaves little to the imagination of the community reader. The assumption is clear—the boy certainly would not lie due to any potential embarrassment. In fact, if the story is a false allegation, the student will still have the protection of police and school officials. There is a strong likelihood that the student will receive no punishment; he will not apologize privately or publicly; and he will retain all rights to attend the school of his choice. The teacher, on the other hand, will be stigmatized for the rest of his career, in or out of the district.

■■

FINAL THOUGHTS

All school districts should be prepared to meet the possibility of a false allegation of teacher sexual misconduct with all prudence. School district administrators must plan for the eventuality of a false allegation of teacher misconduct and be prepared to meet legal guidelines, as well as professional and ethical standards of conduct. Each year, building principals must provide in-service opportunities that include the following:

An overview of problematic teacher behavior.

Legal mandates for sexual harassment prevention.

Proactive strategies for classroom teachers, school counselors, and school administrators.

Clear explanation of school board policy and collective bargaining agreement time lines.

The names of resource personnel whom teachers may contact on an individual basis for further information.

Professional teacher association information regarding teacher indemnification.

Discussion groups that facilitate active problem solving with fellow professionals.

A buddy system for faculty; a colleague to provide support and guidance in daily classroom situations, especially for first-year teachers.

A district-wide system of documentation for teachers' professional notes regarding student disciplinary actions.

Access to community legal experts on sexual abuse allegations.

Access to a trained Title IX officer within the district.

The preamble to the National Education Association Code of Ethics of the Education Profession beautifully expresses this pubic trust for educators to respond fairly: "The educator, believing in the worth and dignity of each human being, recognizes the supreme importance of the pursuit of truth, devotion to excellence and the nurture of democratic principles." All education professionals and paraprofessionals are held to a higher standard of conduct.

■■■■■■■■■■■■■■■■■■■■■■■■■■■■■■■■■■■■■■

IS THERE A WAY TO REGAIN PROFESSIONAL CREDIBILITY AFTER A FALSE ALLEGATION?

In fact, there is no way for a teacher falsely accused of sexual misconduct to regain professional reputation, short of pursuing a civil suit for defamation of character. Some members of the community will hold the teacher innocent, while others will be convinced of the teacher's guilt. A sense of fairness must permeate school district responses to allegations of teacher sexual misconduct. Fairness to students *and* teachers is critical. No true teacher wants to harm students, but no teacher wants to be one false allegation away from losing his or her career, livelihood, and reputation.

■■

TEACHER SURVEY

Please help us begin to document incidents regarding false allegations of teacher misconduct. Take a few moments to answer the following questions. Return the survey via e-mail to mmanos@bradley.edu or mail it to:

Dr. Mary Ann Manos
Bradley University
Peoria, Illinois 61625

Where are you teaching?

Inner City_____ Rural_____ Suburban_____

Private School_____ Public School_____ Charter School_____

Primary_____ Elementary_____ Middle School/Junior High_____

High School_____

Size of your school population_____

Provide a few details of the incident.

What was the one thing you learned through the experience?

What advice would you give to a first-year teacher?

CHAPTER 8

IMPACT CASES

Stare decisis et non quieta movere: to adhere to precedents, and not to unsettle things which are established
—Black's Law Dictionary

■ ■

OVERVIEW

This chapter will help teachers and school administrators to familiarize themselves with recent pertinent court cases. Such cases provide important guidelines for the formulation of sexual harassment policies as well as faculty in-service and student awareness programs. Cases are presented in a manner that facilitates understanding by those who are not legal professionals. In addition, interesting aspects of each case provide discussion topics for faculty development.

■■■

OBJECTIVES

After completing this chapter, the reader should be able to:

1. Define the role of precedent cases in legal interpretation.
2. Identify key areas of liability for teachers and school administrators.

■■

HOW WILL PREVIOUS COURT CASES IMPACT MY SITUATION?

Simply said, precedent court decisions guide future litigation. The body of case law provides a map for judges and attorneys and their clients to follow as new cases are considered. When cases show a factual similarity, following the precedent set in a past case ensures that citizens are treated with equity. Teachers and school administrators must increase their understanding of precedent court decisions delineating teacher and district liability. Schools, teachers, and administrators will be held accountable for federal and state law violations. One area where teachers should never want to see their names printed is in the annals of American case law. Regrettably, the body of civil case law regarding teacher sexual misconduct is growing weekly.

Unfortunately, many educators "fly by the seat of their pants" when day-to-day classroom practice intersects with legal issues, and they fail to protect the rights of their students and themselves. In an effort to support professional development and increase the efficiency of clinical practice for American educators, I have compiled several current legal cases regarding teacher sexual misconduct. The following cases are limited to civil court cases regarding school liability for wrongful actions taken during an investigation. In each case, the plaintiff seeks compensatory or punitive damages from the school district. You should notice that the respondent's list often includes several school administrators, such as superintendents and principals. It is important to remember that the court can and will hold school leadership responsible, both as individuals and in their "official capacity" as school decision makers. It is important to remember that the cases here do not completely focus on the topic of *wrongful* allegations of teacher sexual misconduct. Finally, in most (not all) cases the accused teachers have *admitted* wrongdoing in a criminal court. Teachers who elect to quickly resign in the light of an allegation and who are not charged with any criminal behavior are not represented here. They truly are a silent statistic.

The following citations are but a few of the civil cases impacting current litigation. The cases have not been briefed in true legal fashion. Rather, each has been simply described, keeping the classroom educator and school administrator in mind. Full legal citation is given for those who wish to read the original opinion. Finally, direct connections to the classroom are given beneath each case description.

All selected cases reflect the following list of federal and state mandates for the protection of individual freedoms and rights.

Constitutional rights violations most commonly found in sexual misconduct civil suits include:

1. Title IX–Section 1983 violations
2. Violations of civil rights
3. Denial of equal protection
4. Denial of free access to courts
5. Denial of due process
6. Right to safety in person and bodily integrity

State rights violations usually include:

1. Tort liability–negligence
   a. Failure to adequately train employees
   b. Negligent hiring
   c. Negligent supervision
   d. Gross and deliberate indifference
2. Color of law–state immunity for actions taken as a state actor
3. "Shocks the conscience" standard

■ ■

COURT CASES

1. *Armstrong v. Lamy,* United States District for the District of Massachusetts 938 F. Supp. 1018; 1996 U.S. Dist. Lexis 13633

A former student of the respondent Lamy brings suit against the teacher and school board for acts of sexual abuse perpetrated by the junior high school teacher 20 years earlier. No complaint was made by the student until a repressed memory of the abuse was recalled. The student alleges tort claims of negligence in failure to supervise, inadequate hiring policy, failure to train, and loss of consortium against the teacher, the school district, the municipality, and against the Lamy family members. The student alleges the family of the teacher knew of the late-night sleepovers, the molestation episodes on Lamy family trips, and that school administration should have known of the relationship between the teacher and student because the two appeared in many instances together. Further, the student's wife files for loss of consortium due to the post-traumatic syndrome experienced by her husband, the plaintiff. The court findings are mixed.

Interesting aspects of this case:

- The statute of limitations does not rest on the remoteness of the events.
- The family of the teacher is named as co-respondents. Armstrong argues they are responsible as hosts in the domicile where the alleged abuse takes place.
- The parents of the student gave their permission for 20-30 sleepovers where the teacher and student would be alone.
- The student seems to be a family friend, as he is a musician in a Lamy family musical group.
- The memory of the abuse caused marital discord later in the student's adult life.
- No other allegations toward the teacher surfaced during the court action.

2. *Booth Newspapers v. Kalamazoo School District,* Court of Appeals of Michigan 181 Mich. App. 752; 450 N.W. 2nd 286; 1989 Mich. App. Lexis 666

A news agency filed suit against the school district, the local affiliate of the National Education Association, the district superintendent, the principal, and a teacher because the district withheld information from the newspaper regarding a teacher resignation in connection with an allegation of sexual misconduct. The news agency sought the teacher's name and the names of any students involved, in addition to copies of any tenure changes agreed to by the board. The school district agreed to provide general information devoid of individual names. The court found for the school district and agreed such information is likely to result in personal defamation and stigmatization and can be withheld from news agencies. The court acknowledges that newspapers should not have access to "information pertaining to bare allegations that have not and will not be adjudicated one way or another, given the parties' voluntary settlement . . . [and] the mere fact that an accusation has been made, particularly if it is ultimately found to be untrue, is capable of inflicting embarrassment, humiliation, and destruction of reputation of those named." The court supported the school district's practice of providing information redacted of personal identities.

Interesting aspects of this case:

- A case of defamation of character is possible in a highly publicized, wrongful allegation of teacher sexual misconduct. The school district wants no liability in such a case.
- Newspapers often circumvent seeking information from official sources and go directly to unofficial sources such as the parents of involved students.
- The court found that a case-by-case review is needed to define a right of privacy.

3. *City of Canton, Ohio v. Harris* Supreme Court of the United States 489 U.S. 378; 1989 U.S. Lexis 1200

Although this case doesn't deal with alleged wrongful misconduct by teachers, it holds great interest for the topic at hand. This case involves a city policy that placed sole authority for medical evaluation of prisoners in the hands of an administrator who had received no medical training. The court found this policy was in violation of Section 1983 and posed a liability for the city of Canton. This case is certainly a landmark decision by the United States Supreme Court. School districts, as governmental entities, would do well to heed the court's decision in its expectation for the training of faculty. Faculty members must receive timely training in regard to Title IX sexual harassment definitions and reporting guidelines.

4. *DiSalvio v. Lower Merion High School District,* United States District Court for the Eastern District of Pennsylvania 158 F. Supp. 2nd 553; 2001 U.S. Dist. Lexis 7238

A student manager for the football team alleges that an assistant coach rubbed her leg, knee, and chest, winked at her in a suggestive manner, called her "Honey" and "Sweetheart," patted her buttocks, and slid his hand down the back of her shirt. The coach is also accused of following her into the ladies' room and talking to her while she was in the stall. Finally, the coach is said to have patted another student on the buttocks with a rolled up newspaper during a class period. The student and her parent notified several school personnel of the inappropriate actions by the assistant coach, with no result. The student and parent allege that school administration representatives admonished the student for provoking the behavior and implied the student should remain silent about any conference pertaining to the troublesome behavior by the football coach. The student brings several charges against the coach and school district that include violations of Section 1983. They include negligent supervision, negligent hiring of school employees, and intentional infliction of emotional distress. It is interesting that the student did not initiate a criminal complaint for battery or assault against the coach. Neither did the student bring a legal complaint under Title IX. The court finds in part for the student and in part for the school district, noting that the charge of intentional infliction of emotional distress must rise to the level of "outrageous conduct that would arouse resentment against the actor because his actions exceed all possible bounds of decency." The court found this was the case in the coach's actions.

Interesting aspects of this case:

- Sports programs have a physical culture all their own. Many actions such as pushing, hugging, and patting may easily be misinterpreted. Coaches and school administrators walk a fine line as to appropriate and inappropriate physical behavior toward students in an athletic program. This is certainly an area for intensive professional development.
- The court found the school district had in fact initiated attempts to squelch complaints of sexual harassment by a teacher. This violated qualified immunity for school administrators.

- The student brings reports of actions over several months. Memory delays decrease the teacher's ability to refute allegations or place them in the context of events. Eyewitnesses become crucial in such situations, and the time delay can be critical in reaching the truth of the matter. School officials lost essential time by delaying an official investigation

5. *Doe v. Board of Education of Hononegah Community High School District 207*, United States District Court for the Northern District of Illinois Western Division 833 F. Supp. 1366; 1993 U.S. Dist. Lexis 13881

Doe alleges school administrators and counselors at the high school failed to act on her behalf as required by state and federal law and therefore "fostered an environment of sexual abuse to exist." The incident involves a teacher who perpetrated sexual abuse on students over the span of several years. Several high school counselors and faculty suspected the abuse was factual and reported their concerns to the principal and assistant principal. Doe alleged that school administrators conspired to deprive her of due process, failed to report child abuse to state authorities, failed in their constitutional equal protection obligation, and obstructed her access to the courts. Although the principal, the assistant principal, two counselors, and the district superintendent were aware of the allegations toward the teacher, no official action was taken against him for years. The intervening time span enabled the teacher to abuse several more students. This official delay in action provides a basis for the allegation of official "gross indifference" toward the welfare of students attending the high school. The court found for the plaintiff on several counts.

Interesting aspects of this case:

- States with mandated reporter legislation will not excuse school counselors or educators who fail to report suspected child abuse, even if they attempt to abdicate their responsibility to a higher school authority.
- Restricting free access to the court may involve the failure of school administration to tell parents what their rights are under Title IX.
- The statute of limitations per state may involve different aspects:

  Time begins when the act is perpetrated.

  Time begins when victims know they have suffered harm (e.g. memory delay).

Time begins when students become adults, so they can initiate legal action on their own behalf.

- An official decision not to pursue disciplinary action against
  a teacher may be deemed a conspiracy action if that decision
  is made by several persons in positions of direct supervision
  of the accused.

6. *Doe v. Berkley County School District,* United States District
Court of the District of South Carolina, Charleston Division, 989 F.
Supp. 768; 2997 U.S. Dist. Lexis 21100

Despite repeated warnings by school faculty and administrators,
a student teacher begins a pattern of sexually charged comments toward female high school students in his physical education class. His
improper behavior continued after he was hired as a substitute teacher
in the same district. Two high school students alleged that the teacher
arranged for trysts off school grounds. The parents of the students
approached school administrators and initiated an investigation. This
court action was brought under Title IX and involved the liability of
the school district. The court found that officials for the school did take
appropriate action to stop the abuse of the two students. The court
found for the school distinct.

Intersecting aspects of the case:

- The students told no one until well after the sexual harassment began. One student did not know the other had reported the sexual involvement and therefore did not come
  forward until the investigation had officially started.
- Parents of the students requested an investigation, which the
  school superintendent immediately began.
- Unbelievably, the student teacher's evaluation was exemplary.
  He earned an "excellent" evaluation. The principal, who coun-
  seled him regarding inappropriate comments toward female
  students, did not mention this behavior to the student
  teacher's mentor. Neither did the principal note the incident
  in the student teacher's records.
- School administrators failed to inform distraught parents of
  their Title IX rights or the Office of Civil Rights. This lack of
  information limited their free access to the courts.

7. *Doe v. Gooden,* United States Court of Appeals for the Eighth Circuit 214 F. 3rd 952; 2000 U.S. App. Lexis 12040

School administrators Gooden and Jackson are sued by the parents of six minor children who suffered abuse at the hands of a teacher. The teacher was accused of physical abuse (pushing), verbal abuse (threatening, insulting), and sexual abuse of his students. The parents of the minor children contended that the school administrators should be held liable under Section 1983 as showing deliberate indifference to the teacher actions and thereby violating the students' constitutional rights. The court found for the school administrators, as they had no notice of a pattern of acts committed by the teacher over the 22 years of his teaching service.

Interesting aspects of this case:

- Negligent supervision of faculty may be a legal caveat.
- Interestingly, the plaintiffs allege that school administrators should have known the teacher's potential for abusive sexual behavior due to his sexually harassing interactions with female members of the faculty, as well as his derogatory comments toward female students. Plaintiffs claim this behavior should have been a warning sign to competent administrators. Allowing such conditions to exist results in the condition of "constructive notice," that is, a district *should have known* about harassment but failed to uncover and eliminate it. (Note: Continued professional development with the school faculty regarding sexual harassment in the workplace and the consequences of such behavior might have been the best preventative measure here.)

8. *Fisher v. Independent School District No. 622,* Court of Appeals of Minnesota 357 N.W. 2nd 152; 1984 Minn. App. Lexis 3738

A student alleges sexual contact with an elementary school principal 17 years after the event. The school district immediately begins a process to discharge the principal upon receiving the police report. The principal denies the allegations and contests the discharge as depriving him of due process. Pre-deprivation due process refers to the action taken by school officials prior to placing the accused on suspension or discharging the teacher. The student alleged that the principal perpetuated several molestations against him while he was a student in second through fifth grade. According to the student, the alleged sexual contacts occurred in the principal's private school office. An independent hearing examiner conducted a hearing of fact. Although past teachers of the student did not remember the events as described (two teachers were not available for testimony), the court did not find the remoteness of events as reason to reinstate the principal. In fact, the court writes, "The seriousness of the charges of sexual contact with a student required dismissal, despite the remoteness of the conduct. That remoteness did not result in a denial of due process to appellant." The court found for the school district.

Interesting aspects of this case:

* The principal had no daily records of student visits to his office. If an office log could have been presented to refute the student's account of twice-monthly visits to the principal's office, the case would not have proceeded.

* The student's memory of sexual assault was recalled during a counseling session, 16 years after the fact. Some states will allow the statute of limitations to begin when victims first know they have suffered abuse, perhaps even under hypnosis. The time clock may also begin when victims become adults and can therefore initiate legal action for themselves.

* Precedent cases have, in effect, allowed victims greatly extended time delays prior to reporting sexual assaults by school personnel. The court writes, "By virtue of the nature of the offense—sexual intercourse with a minor student of the district—it may be considered doubtful whether such conduct could ever be too remote in time." (*Johnson v. Independent School District No. 294*, No. 12305, Dist. Ct. Mem. 3rd Judicial Dist, Feb. 12, 1980)

9. *Gebser v. Lago Vista Independent School District,* 524 U.S. 274; 1998 U.S. Lexis 4173

A sexual relationship developed between a high school teacher and his student. The student attended the instructor's book talk sessions, signed up for his independent advanced placement class, and invited the high school English teacher to her home. On several occasions, the teacher took advantage of the isolated settings to initiate a sexual relationship with the student. The student did not report the incidents to school administrators because she was "terrified." She also

explained that the teacher "was the person in Lago administration
... whom I most trusted and he was the one I would have been making the complaint against. If I was to blow the whistle on that, then I
wouldn't be able to have this person as a teacher anymore." Ultimately,
the teacher and student were discovered involved in sexual actions by
the police. The teacher was terminated by the school district and his
teaching certificate revoked by the state of Texas. The student brought
suit under Title IX and sought monetary damages due to the inaction
of school administrators. The court found for the district, holding that
damages may not be recovered for teacher-student sexual harassment
in an implied private action under Title IX unless a school district official, who at a minimum has authority to institute corrective measures
on the district's behalf, has actual notice of and is deliberately indif-
ferent to the teacher's misconduct.

Interesting aspects of this case:

- The student shows signs of consenting to the sexual abuse.
  Of course, this does not absolve the teacher from statutory
  rape charges, but explains why the student did not report the
  improper relationship until caught in an intimate episode.

- Isolated settings, even when part of a school academic schedule, are problematic at best. No classroom should be set aside
  for a one-student class. A library setting with other school
  personnel attending will support both student and teacher
  self-control.

- The district's Title IX officer was the superintendent. It is un-
  likely, in light of other responsibilities expected of the CEO of
  a school district, that sexual harassment issues could receive
  a priority status. This may be the reason the district had not
  distributed an official grievance procedure for lodging sexual
  harassment complaints or a formal anti-harassment policy, as
  required by federal regulations. School districts must make the
  Title IX officer known and accessible to *all* students and faculty. This student felt that no one, other than her abuser,
  would listen to her allegation.

10. *Greendale Education Association v. Greendale School District,*
Court of Appeals of Wisconsin, District One, 2002 Wisc. App. Lexis 1198
    A physical education teacher was accused of inappropriate com-
ments to female students, requiring students to complete stretching

exercises in swimsuits rather than sweat suits, and various other small complaints. The instructor was terminated by the school district. The school and union entered into an arbitration hearing in compliance with the collective bargaining agreement. The hearing officer concluded that although the teacher could be described as insensitive, stubborn, and rude, his behavior did not rise to the level of sexual harassment. The board disagreed and finalized the termination of the teacher. Union attorneys filed suit. The district court supported the school district's termination of the teacher. On appeals, the high court disagreed with the district court's ruling and ordered the teacher to be reinstated.

Interesting aspects of this case:

- Not one of the incidents met the definition of sexual harassing behavior as outlined by the school district's in-house policy.
- The local police declined to press criminal charges against the teacher on the basis of the complaints, yet the school district began termination proceedings.
- Teachers may be operating with an outdated set of social norms, and they need to be given timely information about acceptable behavior within the school setting.

11. *Lillard v. Shelby County Board of Education,* United States Court of Appeals for the Sixth Circuit 76 F. 3rd 716; 1996 U.S. App. Lexis 2578

A girl's soccer team coach is accused of sexual harassment, retaliatory acts toward those who complain, and the battery of one team member. The parents of two students bring a complaint of verbal abuse and vulgarity toward the members of the girls by the coach. The complaints were given in verbal and written form to the athletic director, superintendent, principal, and county board of commissioners. The complaints included several points, but not all complaints included every area of contention. When parents finally brought the case to court, the issues revolved around Title IX and the First Amendment and due process violations as Fourteenth Amendment rights. The court finds for the school board in all but one issue. That issue is the time limitation for Title IX claims (180-day filing period).

Interesting aspects of this case:

- Some disagreements arise relative to the exact reporting period for sexual harassment claims. Relying on Title VII regulations, the court utilized a 180-day reporting period, before claims are time barred. It is important to note that this time limitation is in reference to administrative proceedings, not judicial review.

- Students who say they suffered sexual harassment and verbal and physical abuse continue to play on the team and request to stay in the teacher's academic classes.

- The coach makes personal phone calls to his players. This practice is not encouraged. No phone calls should be made between students and teachers. This practice lends itself to hearsay and wide interpretation.

12. *Peaster Independent School District v. Glodfelty*, Court of Appeals of Texas, Second District, Fort Worth 63 S. W. 3rd 1; 2001 Tex. App. Lexis 3105

This case of two high school teachers accused of sexual misconduct progresses from school district board action to the Texas commissioner of education, and finally, to district court and state appeals court. In this case, a former student alleges teacher sexual misconduct. The student alleged a consensual sexual relationship with both teachers, but declined to report the incident to law enforcement authorities. Instead, the student notified two school board members. After a short interview with the student, the school district superintendent and high school principal recommended that the teachers be "nonrenewed" due to "diminished employee effectiveness." The argument here is that the general knowledge of the allegations, true or not, limited the teachers' effectiveness in the classroom. The claims spread throughout the community. In fact, area newspapers carried the student's story. Immediately, both teachers were placed on administrative leave with pay. At the nonrenewal hearing, no "evidence" other than the sole student account was presented. The student did not appear at the hearing. Additionally, community members who expressed negative opinions about the teachers testified. Consequently, the school board voted to not to renew both teachers. The teachers' employment ended at the close of the academic year. Both teachers filed suit against the school district for wrongful dismissal. The district and appeals court judgment ordered both teachers to be reinstated in the same professional capacity as they were previously employed, with back pay and employment benefits.

Interesting aspects of this case:

- The decision whether to terminate a teacher must be based on the teacher's actions only, not on action by another party.

In this case, what the community members or students said about the educators proved to be the only evidence against the teachers.

- The judge writes, "Fairness dictates against holding teachers' term employment contracts at the mercy of nothing more than an allegation."

- At every level, the Texas teachers lost their appeals until they entered a civil court. Teachers should not be frightened of negative decisions at the district or state board of education levels.

- Teachers do not have to prove their innocence to the school and community. Rather, the school has the burden of reasonable proof of guilt.

- The judge writes, "Such a precedent [of teacher contract nonrenewal resulting from a rumor] would disserve the public interest by discouraging new teachers and preventing our schools from attracting and keeping experienced teachers at a time when there is a critical shortage of those professionals needed to educate our children." This opinion represents a key insight regarding the fragility of a teacher's professional reputation and the volatility of a community rumor mill.

- A student no longer in the district may still lodge a complaint.

- Even if no criminal charge is leveled, a student may still accuse a teacher.

- Each school district's listing of reasons for nonrenewal or firing of teachers must be made common knowledge to the faculty and certainly part of the district collective bargaining agreement.

13. *Stoneking v. Bradford Area School District,* United States Court of Appeals for the Third Circuit 882 F. 2nd 720; 1989 U.S. App. Lexis 15771

A high school band director who perpetrated sexual abuse on a female student over a span of five years pled guilty to the criminal charges. This suit is lodged against the assistant principal, principal, and superintendent of the district that employed him. The suit alleges that school administrators should have known and reacted to protect the student from abuse at the hands of the teacher. Issues include 42 U.S.C. Section 1983 and constitutional due process violations. The

United States Supreme Court remanded this case back to state appeals after the higher court's ruling on a similar case, *Deshaney v. Winnebago*. The plaintiff alleges an environment of hostility toward the student reports of inappropriate behavior by the band director. Further, the plaintiff claims school administrators "failed to take any action to protect the health, safety and welfare of the female student body." Finally, the plaintiff described the school district policies as "defective and deficient" and that those policies led to "reckless indifference to instances of known or suspected sexual abuse of students by teachers, in concealing complaints of abuse and in discouraging students' complaints about such conduct." For example, one female student who lodged an earlier complaint about the band director was required to make a formal apology to the band director in front of the assembled high school band. The court, in *Stoneking*, found for the plaintiffs, finding that the two school administrators could not claim immunity from liability.

Interesting aspects of this case:

- School administrators will not find immunity under "color of law."
- School district policies must be revised with an eye to constitutional rights.
- Competent supervision of school faculty is the school administrators' responsibility and the court's expectation.
- Compulsory attendance laws place students at risk if the school environment is a setting for sexual abuse by school employees, thus a state-created danger.
- Hostile environments for students who complain of sexual harassment will open the school district to legal liability.
- Public apologies from student to teacher will be considered under Title IX as retribution for the initial report and create a "chilling" environment for those who would report sexual harassment in the future.

14. *Tweedall v. Fritz*, United States District Court of South District of Indiana, Evansville Division, 987 F. Supp. 1126; 1997 U.S. Levis 207066: 77 Fair Employment Practices Case.

Tweedall, a teacher accused of sexual misconduct toward several middle school students, was suspended with pay by the school administration. Therefore the suit was brought under the Fourteenth Amendment due-process violations, Title VII and Title IX. Tweedall claims he suffered a denial of due process, sexual harassment, racial discrimination by the school district, and finally, defamation of character. Tweedall failed to meet deadlines for each step of the grievance procedure, although a clear appeals process was described in the collective bargaining agreement. In addition, Tweedall declined a second evidentiary hearing before the school board of trustees, due to a settlement with the school district. The court found for the school district and against the teacher in every claim.

Interesting aspects of this case:

- The sexual misconduct complaint was not initiated by the students involved, but by a teacher who "overheard" student discussion of the alleged events.

- The constructive discharge (working conditions so intolerable as to force a reasonable employee to leave) constituted a stigmatization of the teacher.

- A teacher may be provided little pre-deprivation due process. For the protection of students, a verbal notification of immediate suspension was accepted by the court as a fair and appropriate action toward the teacher by the school district.

- The judge described teachers as those who are in a "unique position of trust and authority," therefore held to a higher standard of responsibility in the community.

- The teacher-district settlement agreement provided for a change in teaching assignment, allowed a statement of charges and evidence to be placed in the teacher's file, and required the teacher to attend counseling prior to being placed in a teaching assignment. The agreement also initiated a suspension without pay until reassigned. Tweedall agreed to each condition.

- The new teaching assignment proved unsuccessful. The teacher left the classroom on disability leave due to an emotional breakdown. He left his new teaching assignment after one day in the classroom.

- Teachers must be sure to meet all collective bargaining deadlines for filing a grievance.

15. *Wilson v. Webb,* United States Court of Appeals for the Sixth District 2000 U.S. App. Lexis 23585

Two high schools students file suit against a teacher who sexually abused both students. Webb, superintendent of the county school district and Stice, the high school principal, are also named in the liability suit. Students allege that school administrators showed deliberate indifference to the improper actions of the teacher. Legal issues include violations of Title IX and due-process protections as well as state laws. Over the span of a school year, the teacher perpetrated sexual abuse upon two students. The case involves testimony for and against the teacher by students, therapists, faculty, nonprofessional staff, and administrators. The district court jury found the teacher liable for his actions and awarded the girls hefty compensatory and punitive damages. One girl was awarded approximately $151,000. The other student received approximately $300,000. The principal and superintendent were not found to be negligent in their official handling of the investigation. They were awarded compensation for attorneys' fees and court costs.

Interesting aspects of this case:

- Applies the "shocks the conscience" standard to sexual abuse of students.
- The jury takes the perception of the student over the intent of the teacher.
- No evidence regarding prior student behavior is allowed.

GLOSSARY
OF ESSENTIAL TERMS

Note: Readers must be aware that state mandates, education codes, and local law enforcement vary greatly in scope, detail, intent, and timelines. Although the following definitions are very broad, they will help construct a general understanding of allegations regarding teacher sexual misconduct. Your state and local mandates and/or community expectations may or may not be identical to what is reported here. It is the teacher's professional responsibility to know the laws, customs, and policies in effect for their specific school placement.

Accidental contact: Contact outside of the teacher's official capacity (such as off campus) with a minor who is not a student.

Accused: A person accused of a criminal offense.

Advisory personnel: Certified school employees who provide counseling services.

Aggravated criminal sexual abuse: Sexual penetration (or the threat of sexual penetration) by use of force or threat; victim is underage, unable to understand the act, or a family member. Accused is an adult and holds a position of trust. The following conditions may apply:

- A weapon other than a firearm is displayed or discharged (or the victim *believed* there to be a weapon)

- Victim has bodily harm
- Victim's life is threatened
- Incident occurs in the commission of another felony
- Victim is 60 or older
- Victim is handicapped
- Victim is drugged
- Victim is of limited mental competence
- Victim is under age 13, while accused is under adult age

Aggravated sexual assault: A wide range of victimizations, separate from rape or attempted rape; includes verbal threats, attacks, or attempted attacks, generally involving unwanted sexual contact, that may or may not involve force. This is a felony charge. It may be committed without touching.

Aggravated sexual battery: A felony charge that includes any unlawful touching of another that is without justification or excuse. The incident may include rape, indecent liberties, child molestation, or sodomy.

Assigned authority: Authority implied from holding a particular position, such as clergy, teacher, and an employer. For students, this would include paraprofessionals, teacher aides, custodial workers, coaches, school administrators, and hall or study monitors.

Bodily harm: Refers to any physical harm and includes sexually transmitted disease, pregnancy, and impotence.

Buckley Amendment: Now known as the Family Educational Rights and Privacy Act of 1974, this legislation secured the rights of parents to view cumulative student files as well as pertinent teacher rating or observation.

Caregiver: Any person caring for a child or adolescent in parental role or substituting for the parental role.

Child abuse: The physical injury or neglect, mental injury, sexual abuse, sexual molestation, or maltreatment of a child under the age of 18.

Civil Rights Act of 1991: Legislators amended Title VII to permit victims to add punitive damages for mental distress due to sexual harassment. Victims may request back pay, front pay, and actual out-of-pocket expenses. Enforced by the Equal Employment Opportunity Commission, cases may be resolved through intergovernmental agreement and cooperation with the school district, or action through the U.S. Department of Justice, seeking injunctive relief. Remedies may include the award of monetary damages, compensation for wages and job-connected losses, reinstatement and/or promotion, and compensation for attorney's fees.

Civil suits: Court action brought to gain or recover individual or civil rights or to obtain redress for an alleged noncriminal injustice. Noncriminal judicial action surrounding teacher sexual misconduct episodes tend to center on specific issues. They include sexual harassment of students, negligent hiring, negligent supervision, constitutional violation for denial of civil rights, the right to safety and liberty, equal protection under the law, free access to the courts, and defamation or slander.

Coercion: The use of extortion, bribes, threats, or intimidation to gain cooperation or compliance.

Collective bargaining agreement: The contractual agreement between a union and the school board.

"Color of law": Action or power clothed with the authority of state.

Compensatory damages: Also called "actual damages"; money that may be recovered in the courts to compensate losses by a person who has suffered loss, detriment, or injury to person, property, or rights.

Compulsive: Behavior that cannot be controlled; an irresistible impulse.

Confidentiality: Family Education Rights and Privacy Act of 1974 restricts access to a student's records to certain parties.

Consent: Agreement for participation in sexual behavior. (Note: minor children are never considered to have given consent.)

The following conditions apply:

- Participants must understand what is proposed

- Participants must be of age and have the maturity level and experience level to understand

- Participants must have knowledge and understanding of social standards of behavior

- Participants must be aware of consequences or alternatives

- There is an assumption of free will in decision making; a power balance exists

- Participants must exhibit mental competence

Constructive discharge: When a reasonable employee is forced to resign because working conditions are intolerable.

Constructive notice: Behavior that should be a warning sign to competent administrators, such as sexually harassing interactions with female or male members of the faculty, as well as derogatory comments toward students; *that is, a district should have known about sexual harassment but failed to uncover and eliminate it.* Continued professional development with the school faculty regarding sexual harassment in the workplace and the consequences of such behavior is the best preventative measure.

Criminal: Dealing with the law of crime; commission of a crime.

Criminal sexual assault: Sexual penetration by use of force or threat, victim is underage, unable to understand the act, or a family member. The accused is an adult and in a position of trust.

Defamation: Holding a person up to ridicule, scorn, or contempt in a respectable and considerable part of the community; includes both slander and libel; a statement that exposes a person to contempt, hatred, or ridicule.

Delayed memory: Memory of injury suffered during childhood sexual abuse that is recalled for the first time during adulthood.

Disciplinary action: A response by school board members or their representative that would punish or incur a penalty against an employee.

Discovery: Pretrial devices that can be used by one party to obtain facts and information about the case from the other party; opportunity one party has to see the evidence against them.

Documentation: Teacher professional notes and papers; written observations.

Due process: An orderly proceeding in which a person is served with notice and has an opportunity to be heard and to enforce and protect his or her rights. The constitutional right that protects persons from arbitrary action; teachers must be afforded a fair procedure for hearing and responding to the charges that endanger their continued employment.

Due Process Clause, U.S. Constitution, Fourteenth Amendment: Due process of law implies the right of a person to be heard and to have the right to refute every material fact that bears on the question of life, liberty, or property (employment). Teachers who lose employment as a result of wrongful allegations of sexual misconduct may seek relief from due process violations. Remedies include compensatory and punitive damages along with injunctive relief.

Emotional distress: Intentional infliction of emotional distress happens when a person has suffered ongoing harassment; for example, when an institutions shows indifference.

Equal Protection Clause—U.S. Constitution, Fourteenth Amendment: Cases brought under this federal protection includes public institutional liability for intentional sexual harassment. Also included here is the issue of equal access to remedies in courts of law. School employees who do not provide accurate information regarding appeal of school policy decisions restrict equal access. Remedies include compensatory and punitive damages along with injunctive relief.

Evidentiary hearing: A hearing during which evidence is presented for evaluation; a meeting comprising school board members, school administrators, the accused teacher, and legal representation for the purposes of placing all evidence (i.e., those facts that are necessary for the final determination of employment status) into consideration.

Exhibitionism: Public exposure of breast, buttocks, or genitals.

Exploitation: Conduct that allows, employs, authorizes, permits, induces, or encourages others to engage in activities that are not in their best interest in order to achieve self-gratification.

Federal court: A court that hears issues regarding U.S. constitutional or federal statutes violations only.

Felony: A criminal act that would subject the party to imprisonment (note: many state penal or criminal codes have various classes of felonies, with varying sentences for each class).

Fiduciary relationships: A person having the duty, created by his or her undertaking, to act primarily for another's benefit; founded on a trust or confidence.

Fondling: Touching the genitals, buttocks, or breasts of others for sexual gratification.

Force or threat of force: The use or threat of violence that may include the accused threatening another person other than the victim when the victim is physically restrained or physically confined.

Frottage: Bumping, touching, or rubbing against others for sexual gratification without their knowledge or consent (note: minor children are never considered to have given consent).

Grooming behavior: Engagement strategies whereby harassers gain the special trust of the victim or take advantage of special relationships that already exist.

Hostile environment: Applies when the harassing behavior of anyone in the workplace causes the workplace to become hostile, intimidating, or offensive. An environment that occurs when unwelcome conduct of a sexual nature is so severe, persistent, or pervasive that it affects one's ability to participate in or benefit from a person's work, education program, or activity, or creates an intimidating, threatening, or abusive educational environment.

Ideation: The forming of ideas; fantasies.

Immoral: Actions that do not conform to principles of right conduct.

Improper sexual conduct: Any intentional touching or fondling of the victim, either directly or though clothing, for the purpose of sexual gratification.

Indemnification: Contract to which one person secures (insures) another against loss or for some responsibility assumed by another.

Injunctive relief: A remedy issued or granted by a court at the suit of a complainant.

In loco parentis: Schools serve in the place of a parent; charged with parental rights and responsibilities; the official capacity and responsibility of teachers to protect and instruct children.

Intervention: Actions that correct, control, or prevent a problem.

Intimidation: To frighten another in order to gain compliance. Examples could include verbal threats, physical danger, or fear of reprisal or violence.

Legal representation: Employment of an attorney.

Liability: A legal responsibility.

Lolita: A fictional character; a child who exhibits seductive behavior toward an adult.

Malfeasance: Evildoing; any wrongful act or any wrongful conduct that affects performance of official duty; an act for which there is no authority or warrant of law but which a person ought not do at all; an unlawful act.

Mandated reporter: Persons who, in the performance of their occupational duties, have reasonable cause to suspect that a child has suffered harm as a result of child abuse or neglect, shall, by law immediately report the incident to the child protection agencies.

Misconduct: A transgression of some established and definite rule of action; a forbidden act; a dereliction of duty; implies willful or wanton disregard of standards of behavior.

Misfeasance: Improper performance of a lawful act.

Moral turpitude: An act of baseness, vileness, or one that gravely violates moral sentiment or accepted moral standards of community and is culpable in some criminal offenses.

National Labor Relations Act: This law protects teachers who are disciplined or terminated because they attempted to hold meetings around student allegations of teacher sexual misconduct. The National Labor Relations Act protects employees who undertake to improve sexual harassment polices within the school district.

Negligent hiring: Charged when the school district fails in its responsibility to hire persons of high moral standing.

Negligent supervision: Charged when school supervisory personnel fail to provide protection from sexual harassment.

Nonfeasance: Failure to perform a required duty.

Official capacity: Duties within the scope of one's employment; actions taken by employees under the auspices of their institutional responsibilities; a way to sue the public entity that the official represents.

Parent notification: All letters, telephone calls, or conferences with parents.

Pariah: An outcast.

Pattern of misconduct: School districts may be required to show a history of inappropriate behavior by the teacher prior to dismissal. School districts may consider past teacher effectiveness and prior complaints from fellow faculty, parents, or students. Also includes any prior incidents that may show misconduct. Examples may include comments made to fellow faculty members, comments made to minors other than students, or any suspicious contact with any child.

Polygraph: A mechanism for recording variations in body response used to validate personal accounts in criminal investigations.

Post-deprivation: Action taken against the teacher by the school district after the loss of employment or suspension of teaching duties.

Predatory criminal sexual assault of a child: Sexual penetration when the accused is 17 years old or older and the victim is under 13. Includes the following conditions:

- The use of firearms
- Bodily harm, permanent disability, or threatening life
- The use of a drug.

Pre-deprivation: Action taken against the teacher by the school district prior to loss of employment or suspension of teaching duties.

Professional ethics: An enforced code of uniform rules and behavioral standards by means of which members of the profession are informed of acceptable behavior; concerns public acts by persons in their professional roles.

Property right: The right to specific property whether it is personal or real property, tangible or intangible. Teachers under continuing contract have a property right to continued employment.

Protected Liberty—U.S. Constitution, 14th Amendment: U. S. citizens have a right to a protected liberty of bodily integrity. Used in sexual abuse allegations, this describes the right to be protected from physical harm. In loco parentis includes the responsibility of the schools, as temporary parents, to protect students from physical harm. Remedies include compensatory and punitive damages along with injunctive relief.

Punitive damages: Monetary awards as punishment for outrageous conduct or to deter future transgressions.

Quid pro quo: a relationship in which something is given or withheld in exchange for something else (sexual behavior). Usually describes improper use of power in a "something given or something withheld in exchange" relationship. Quid pro quo sexual harassment involves:

- Submission for sexual demands that are made either explicitly or implicitly as a term or condition of employment or advancement
- Submission for sexual demands that are made a basis for decisions affecting a person's employment or academic standing

Rape: Forced sexual intercourse; includes psychological coercion as well as physical force.

Reasonable action: Obligation to meet the "reasonable person" standard as expected in a court of law; a "reasonable woman" standard may be used in cases of alleged sexual harassment.

Remediation: The opportunity for teachers to improve their teaching effectiveness under direct supervision by school administrators prior to termination.

Section 504 of the Rehabilitation Act of 1973—P.L. 93-112: This mandate requires school administrators to carefully consider disciplinary action against any disabled student who might be involved in teacher harassment.

Sexual assault: A wide range of victimizations, including grabbing, fondling, verbal threats; a wide range of victimizations, separate from rape or attempted rape. Includes verbal threats, attacks, or attempted attacks generally involving unwanted sexual contact that may or may not involve force. This is a felony charge. It may be committed without touching.

Sexual battery: A felony charge that includes any unlawful touching of another which is without justification or excuse. The incident may include rape, fondling, indecent liberties, child molestation, or sodomy.

Sexual conduct: Any intentional or knowing touching or fondling by the victim or the accused, either directly or through clothing, of the sex organs, anus, or breast of the victim or accused, or any part of the body of a child under 13 years of age, for the purpose of sexual gratification or arousal of the victim or the accused.

Sexual gratification: Arousal of the victim or the accuser, either directly or though clothing.

Sexual harassment: Unwanted sexual attention; unreciprocated verbal and nonverbal sexual behaviors may include the distribution of obscene or pornographic materials.

Governmental categories include the following:

- Gender harassment
- Sexual coercion

- Seductive behavior
- Sexual bribery
- Sexual assault

Sexualized behavior: Compulsive behavior that is self-abusive including masturbation, self-fondling, or rubbing against furniture; behavior that violates social norms.

Sexually Abusive (Aggressive) Children and Youth (S.A.C.Y.): Children who exhibit sexually problematic behavior; children who commit sexual assaults, rapes, and molestation on other young children. When confronted, children engaging in sexually aggressive behavior typically blame the behavior on others or angrily deny their behavior.

Sexually aggressive behavior: Sexual activity between two persons that is not consensual and includes physical/psychological force or coercion toward another. Implies a "power imbalance" between perpetrator and the victim. Sexual aggression may include the following:

- Fondling
- Frottage
- Penetration
- Verbal abuse

Sexually aggressive children and adults often blame the victim, who may or may not exhibit visible injury or mental harm.

"Shocks the conscience" standard: Teacher actions so grossly excessive as to be shocking to the conscience of a reasonable person; those actions violate substantive due-process rights, without regard to state remedies. Punitive damages against the teacher will be based on this question: Did the teacher's actions amount to "brutal and inhumane abuse of official power, literally shocking the conscience of reasonable persons?" Sexual misconduct perpetrated by educators always meets the "shocks the conscience" standard.

State court: A court that hears issues regarding state constitutional or statute violations only.

State education codes: These vary from state to state. Some states include a statement of professional ethics that allows termination or suspension of teacher certificates for moral turpitude or immortality based on community standard.

State laws: May include antidiscrimination statutes that apply to students, school district administrators, and teachers. Fair employment practice guidelines vary considerable from state to state. Equal Employment Opportunity Commission policies are often found in state Fair Employment Practice guidelines. Remedies and time lines differ from state to state.

Substantive evidence: Viewing the evidence, on the whole, reasonable minds would reach the same conclusion.

Suit: A proceeding in a court of law brought by a plaintiff and answered by a respondent.

Termination: The end of all employment opportunities within a district.

Title VII of the Civil Rights Act of 1964: This legislation, enforced by the Equal Employment Opportunity Commission, permits victims of employment discrimination based upon race, color, national origin, religion, or sex to collect compensatory damages for sexual harassment (a form of sexual discrimination). Several policy guidance papers are available for school administrators from the Equal Employment Opportunity Commission. Remedies may include injunctive relief and compensatory and punitive damages, within limitations.

Title IX of the Education Amendments of 1972: This legislation covers all institutions receiving federal aid. This federal statute is enforced by the Office of Civil Rights and protects victims of sex discrimination. The revised 2001 Office of Civil Rights policy guidance on sexual harassment situations provides standards of determining an institution's liability. The Office of Civil Rights provides guidelines for grievance procedure, filing a complaint, investigation procedure, program definitions and limitations, time limits for filing, confidentiality issues, and compliance reviews of school district. Remedies include monetary damages for suffering and emotional distress, future medical or therapeutic costs, attorney's fees, wages and job-related losses, reinstatement or promotion, tuition refunds, and injunctive relief requiring schools to change policy or training policy. It is important to note that even if plaintiffs lose in a court decision, they may file a complaint with the Office of Civil Rights.

Title 42 under the United States Code, Section 1983: This law protects anyone acting "under color of law" from depriving individuals of any right secured by the U.S. Constitution. Section 1983 allows plaintiffs to be heard in a federal court. Allegations of harassment or personal injury by state employees in the performance of their jobs hold both individuals and institutions liable. Remedies include compensatory and punitive damages along with injunctive relief.

Tort: A private or civil wrong or injury; its three aspects include a legal duty, a breach of duty, and damage as a result.

Transference: When students in need of emotional support adopt feelings for their teachers that are similar to the feelings they have had in a prior close relationship, such as a parent.

Victim: Any person harmed by another.

Voyeurism: Obtaining sexual gratification from seeing another person disrobed.

Witness: A credible person who sees or perceives a thing; a spectator.

Wrongful discharge: Termination for refusal to tolerate sexual harassment.

INDEX

About the Author

MARY ANN MANOS, a 30-year veteran of the classroom, is presently Director, Bradley University Institute for Gifted and Talented Youth.